Boro Baba...

Ustad Alauddin Khan

Family Pride

Boro Baba...Ustad Alauddin Khan

Sahana Gupta née Khan

Lustre Press
Roli Books

Dhyanesh Khan

Grandson of Baba Alauddin Khan; second son of Ali Akbar Khan, a renowned sarode player and a successful teacher of music; was a lecturer in Rabindra Bharati University. The entire collection of pictures in this book is his effort and prompted his daughter, the author, to give shape to this biography.

Dedication

My relationship with my father blossomed when I was in my teens. He began treating me as a friend instead of a daughter and shared his concerns about work and business. It was during this time that I realized what his most prized possession was – a vast collection of photographs and other papers documenting his grandfather's (Boro Baba's) phenomenal achievements. I was struck by the awe and respect his grandfather inspired in my father. It was not merely the familial bond which mattered to him. Instead, he bowed his head before the immensity of the old man's talent, the trajectory of his eventful life, and his immeasurable contribution to the world of Indian music. Viewing Boro Baba through my father's eyes, I became aware of the fact that I had inherited a tremendous legacy and it was my duty to uphold it throughout my life.

It was my father's dream to put his grandfather's life together in a manner which would be a fitting tribute to his genius. Unfortunately, he passed away before he could fulfill this desire and left me behind to complete what he had started. It was a mammoth task and the first step I took was to organize a couple of local exhibitions that showcased Boro Baba's life through a series of photographs. The enthusiastic response these exhibitions generated, motivated me to envisage something far larger in scale. In the midst of my father's collection of photographs, I had come across a handwritten manuscript, in which Boro Baba had pieced together invaluable anecdotes about his life as well as his musical odyssey. I then began looking for a platform that would enable me to give the manuscript a genuine shape and form. This book, detailing the rise of this legendary personality, signifies the end of my quest.

I dedicate this book to my guru, my father. Without his hard work, principles, dreams and love, the completion of this work would not have been possible.

Acknowledgements

I have tapped numerous sources while writing this book. First and foremost, I would like to acknowledge my debt to the handwritten manuscript of Ustad Alauddin Khan which gave me unimaginable insights into the mind of the genius and his life. I would also like to thank Mobarak Hussain Khan for giving me permission to use and adapt freely from his books *Ustad Alauddin Khan – The Legend in Music* and *Ustad Alauddin Khan O Tar Patraboli*. Chandan Chakraborty's webpage was also extremely informative. I am grateful to Usha Shetty, Manisha Abraham and H. V. Vishwanath for their help in constructing the narrative of the book. I would also like to extend my thanks to Pramod and Priya Kapoor for publishing the book and the editors of Roli Books (Dipa Chaudhuri, Priyanka and Simar) for their continuous support and additions in the book.

ISBN: 978-81-7436-386-2

Text: © Sahana Gupta 2009
Translation (pages 18-22): Indrani Bhattacharya
Photographs and documents:
© Sahana Gupta private collection except
Getty Images: pages 42-43
Corbis: pages 30, 33, 34-35
Shelley Mazumdar: pages 38, 64, 71 (bottom), 72 (left top & bottom), 78 (right), 83 (top), 88 (right), 127 (top left & right)

Published in India by
Roli Books in arrangement
with Roli & Janssen BV
M-75 Greater Kailash-II (Market)
New Delhi - 110 048, India.
Phone: ++91-11-40682000, 29212782
Fax: ++91-11-29217185
E-mail: info@rolibooks.com
Website: www.rolibooks.com

Editor: Simar Puneet
Design: Sneha Pamneja
Layout: Naresh L. Mondal
Production: Naresh Nigam

Printed and bound in Singapore

Contents

Foreword

by Annapurna Devi

Annapurna Devi

It can be rightfully said that she walked in her father, Baba Alauddin's footsteps. Her contribution to our musical heritage has been immense.

I always remember Baba with a combination of respect, awe and love. I possess deep *shraddha* (respect) for him from my very childhood. He was different from anyone else I had met in my life. He was simple, ego less, truthful, full of love and respect for people but, above all, he was an embodiment of compassion when it came to poor people. I was always close to him and he, in turn, loved me dearly.

While I was a student, I never dared ask Baba what his favourite *ragas* were, nor did Baba ever speak about his performances. All my time was spent in learning and practising in order to perfect my technique. However, it would be of interest to know that Baba himself created many ragas such as Hemant, Manj-Khamaj, Hem-Behag, Shubhavati and Yaman-Manj that have transcended the boundaries of stereotypical *gharanas*.

Baba first taught vocal music (*dhrupad*) to Dada, Ali Akbar Khan saheb, and me. Later, when I was learning the *sitar* from him, he told me, 'I want to teach you my guru's *vidya* because you have no greed. To learn, you have to have infinite patience and a calm mind. I feel that you can preserve my guru's gift because you love music. However, you will have to give up playing the *sitar*, an instrument liked by connoisseurs as well as commoners. The *surbahar*, on the other hand, will be appreciated only by discerning listeners, who understand the depth of music, who intuitively feel music. The commoner might throw tomatoes at you. So what is your decision?' I was dumbfounded. 'I will do as per your *adesh* (bidding),' was my instant response.

I do not play all the instruments that Baba played. I only learnt to sing and to play the *sitar* and the *surbahar*. However, I do teach the flute, the *sarode* and other instruments.

For me, music is akin to worship. Baba used to say that one could reach God through music. He also told me that if ever the need arose, I would be able to earn my living through music and be economically independent.

I practise what Baba taught me as a form of meditation. I work at doing justice to what he taught me. He used to say that every note should touch one's soul. This is extremely difficult and requires eternal *sadhana*. It is a process of total surrender, of submerging one's ego.

I believe that learning any instrument is a very demanding task – requiring time, commitment and untiring effort. I have observed that in our society, as long as a woman is not married, she may be able to give what it takes to become a great instrumentalist. However, after marriage there are other demands on her time and she is not able to continue her rigorous practise of music (*riyaz*). I don't think there are any physical limitations that come in the way of a woman mastering any instrument. All she needs is a burning desire, a right guru, discipline and determination.

As far as taboos are concerned, let me share with the reader what happened with my sister. Baba taught her vocals with much love. He was very disturbed when she was not allowed to sing by her conservative in-laws. Due to this experience, he was in a dilemma about whether to teach me music or not. But I used to listen to and remember what he taught Dada. One day, Baba went to the market and Dada was practising his lessons on the *sarode*. Dada made a mistake and I was correcting him. I was so involved in the music that I did not notice Baba had returned. Suddenly I became aware of his presence. He was right behind me and I got scared. But instead of scolding me, Baba called me to his room and gave me a tanpura. This was the beginning of my *taleem* (instruction).

There was no difference in the way I was taught music, though I was a woman. As a matter of fact, Dada and I were given the same *taleem*. I think music knows no gender differences. Emotional and aesthetic expression have more to do with the artist's personality than with gender. An introspective artist might go for *sur* and *alaap* while an extrovert might opt for *laykari*.

Baba was also deeply religious but ecumenical in spirit. He worshipped Sharda Ma and also read *namaz* five times a day. He was witty and humorous.

One day, a visitor came to see him while he was watering some plants outside the house. The visitor mistook him for a gardener and ordered him to inform Baba of his arrival. Baba quietly went inside and reappeared and introduced himself as Baba!

As a guru he was most exacting, a purist and a perfectionist. He helped his students develop their own style and encouraged them to imbue music with their own feelings. That is why the same phrase played by Dada and Pandit Ravi Shankar would sound different.

Baba had the attributes of an ideal guru, one who had patience and the vision to bring out the best in individual students.

As a musician, he had mastered many instruments. This list is already mentioned. He was also the first one to introduce the concept of an orchestra in Indian music. Certain renditions were so intense and moving that the audience could hardly control their tears. I remember even the Maharaja of Maihar had to walk out of one of the concerts since he didn't want his people to see their ruler so overcome with emotion.

In spite of Nawab Bahadur Hamid Ali Khan of Rampur recommending Baba to Ustad Wazir Khan saheb, the Ustad tested Baba's patience, motivation and the intensity of his desire to learn from him for over two years. During this period, Baba used to sit outside the closed doors of the Ustad's chambers, listen to the *taleem* imparted by the Ustad to his disciples inside, memorize the instructions and practise them all night.

It was only after the Ustad received a telegram from our home saying that my mother had tried to commit suicide, that he became aware of Baba's commitment and sacrifice, and earnestly started teaching him.

After mastering Ustad Wazir Khan saheb's teachings, Baba became the court musician of Maihar estate in Madhya Pradesh. He spent the rest of his life there – teaching, composing and playing music.

Besides what Baba had learnt from Ustad Wazir Khan saheb, he had also mastered various instruments from different experts of his time.

With his rich repertoire and vast body of musical knowledge, he evolved a new style which came to be known as the Maihar *gharana*, with its roots in the Senia *gharana* of Mian Tansen, carried forward by Ustad Wazir Khan saheb who was a direct descendant of Mian Tansen.

The Maihar *gharana* has brought to Indian classical music its own special touch. In the Maihar *gharana*, the usual style of presentation is that of *dhrupad*, where the *alaaps* are systematic, slow, dignified and serene without the *khatkaas* and *murkis*. The *jod ang* has intricate *laykari*, rhythmic patterns and the *alaap* and *jhalas* have plenty of variations without any gimmicks. Through a presentation, the purity of a given *raga* is sustained. The *gats* of the Maihar *gharana* are not confined to *teental*.

Baba spent over four decades of his life in Maihar – playing, teaching and sharing his divine gift of music. His disciples include an impressive line-up of some of the front-ranking instrumentalists of the twentieth century. Each is a world class musician and the finest exponent of a musical instrument: Padma Vibhushan Ustad Ali Akbar Khan (*sarode*), Bharat Ratna Pandit Ravi Shankar (*sitar*), the late Pandit Pannalal Ghosh (flute), Padma Bhushan Pandit V. G. Jog (violin), Padma Bhushan Pandit Nikhil Banerji (*sitar)* and many others. What is more, Baba transformed some chamber or folk instruments into concert-worthy ones.

Above all, Baba was perhaps the most secular individual I have known in my life.

Padma Bhushan Dr. Annapurna Devi
Mumbai

The Foundation

1

The history of our grandparents is remembered not with rose petals but in the laughter and tears of children and their children's children. It is into us that the lives of grandparents have gone. It is in us that their history becomes a future.

—Charles and Ann Morse

Maihar was a place I always looked forward to visiting as a child. In the company of my paternal grandmother and great-grandmother, my holidays at Madina Bhawan were very enjoyable; away from the hustle and bustle of Calcutta. My grandmother, Zubeda Khan, introduced me to my great-grandfather – Ustad Alauddin Khan – by stopping to pay homage at his tomb, built outside Madina Bhawan, even before we set foot in the premises. As a child, all I did was follow suit, bowing my head to this great man whose immensity hasn't stopped unfolding till date. But his lifestyle intrigued me. His living room and bedroom were the focal point in Madina Bhawan. The walls exhibited a fascinating medley of photographs, including snapshots of the family, his gurus, religious teachers as well as interesting advertisements and newspaper cuttings. The bedroom had a bed and a hookah, characteristic of a typical eighteenth-century refined lifestyle. These remains of the past piqued my curiosity and made me want to know more about my Boro Baba ('Boro' means bigger/older and Baba means father, in Bengali).

I would listen mesmerized, to the stories my grandmother would tell about Boro Baba, and when in Maihar, I would be able to interpret

Baba Alauddin Khan.

FACING PAGE:

Madina Bhawan, Boro Baba's house in Maihar, Madhya Pradesh.

Built on a piece of land gifted by the Maharaja of Maihar, the house was designed by Boro Baba himself and named after his wife, Madina Begum.

RIGHT:

Boro Baba.

This portrait of Boro Baba has found its way into many archives.

BELOW:

Zubeda Khan with her children.

(L to R): Ameena Perera, Aashish Khan, Zubeda Khan, Dhyanesh Khan. Front row: Amaresh Khan and Pranesh Khan.

FACING PAGE:

A collage of memories.

1. Boro Baba (centre) after he returned from a tour of Europe.
2. Boro Baba's bedroom, just as it was when he was alive.
3. Boro Baba's grandchildren with their mother (L to R): Amaresh Khan, Pranesh Khan, Aashish Khan, Dhyanesh Khan, their mother Zubeda Khan and Ameena Perera.
4. Madina Begum (centre) in Madina Bhawan with her grandchildren. (L to R): Aashish Khan, Kirit Khan, Ameena and Dhyanesh Khan.
5. Boro Baba with Boro Ma.
6. Ali Akbar Khan and his wife Zubeda Khan.
7. Aashish Khan, Pranesh Khan, Zubeda Khan, Ali Akbar Khan, Ameena Perera and Dhyanesh Khan.

these incidents within the proper ambience. Once, when I was a little older, I saw Baba (my father, Dhyanesh Khan) in the midst of a huge pile of photographs strewn around him. Inquisitive as I was, I sat beside him and made him describe each picture. This made it easier to visualize all the tales my grandmother had narrated.

I wish that I had met Boro Baba, but that was not to be. The pages that follow speak of Boro Baba's life pieced together from his own handwritten manuscript, stories that I have heard from my grandmother, grandfather, Baba and many others who have had the fortune of knowing the legend in his lifetime.

1

2

3

4

5

6

7

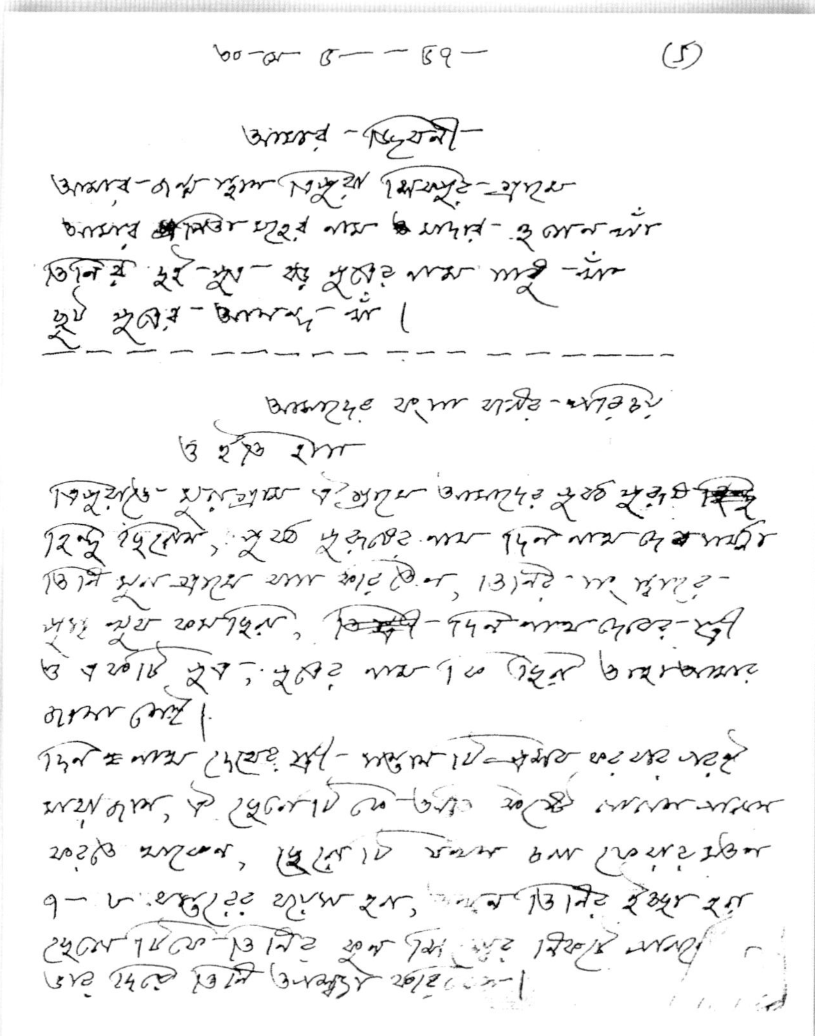

Baba Alauddin's handwritten autobiography.

Boro Baba's manuscript titled 'My Autobiography' is dated 30 May, 1957. On this first page, he talks about the "history and identity" of his geneology. "The name of my grandfather is Madar Hussain Khan...my forefathers were Hindus" he says. He then describes his ancestor - a "man of great learning" - Dinanath Dev Sharma, who "gave up the material world to practise religious austerities."

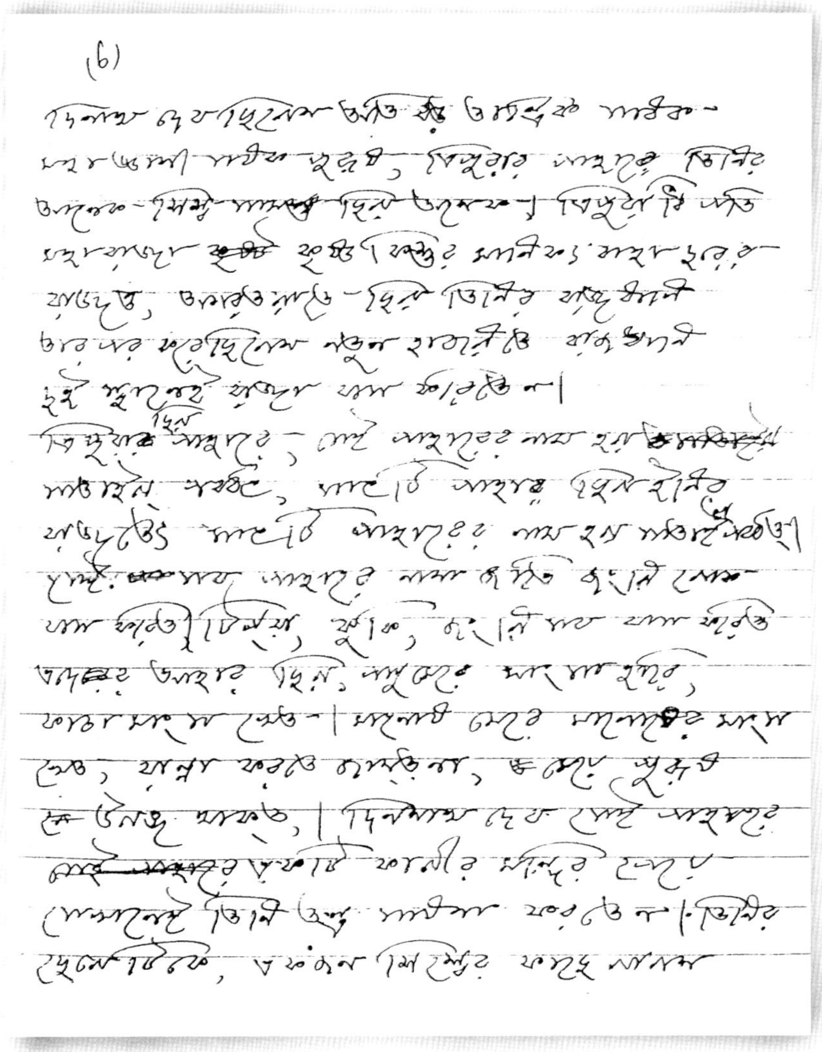

Tripura Legacy.

Dinanath Dev Sharma became a famous holy man and even received a royal honour from the Tripura king. Boro Baba describes the hills of Tripura saying, "There were seven big hills all around and the area was known as Santayl Parbat. The hills were inhabited by tribals who hunted and ate raw flesh - sometimes eating human flesh too." Dinanath Dev found a Kali temple in these hills and settled there to meditate and practise tantra.

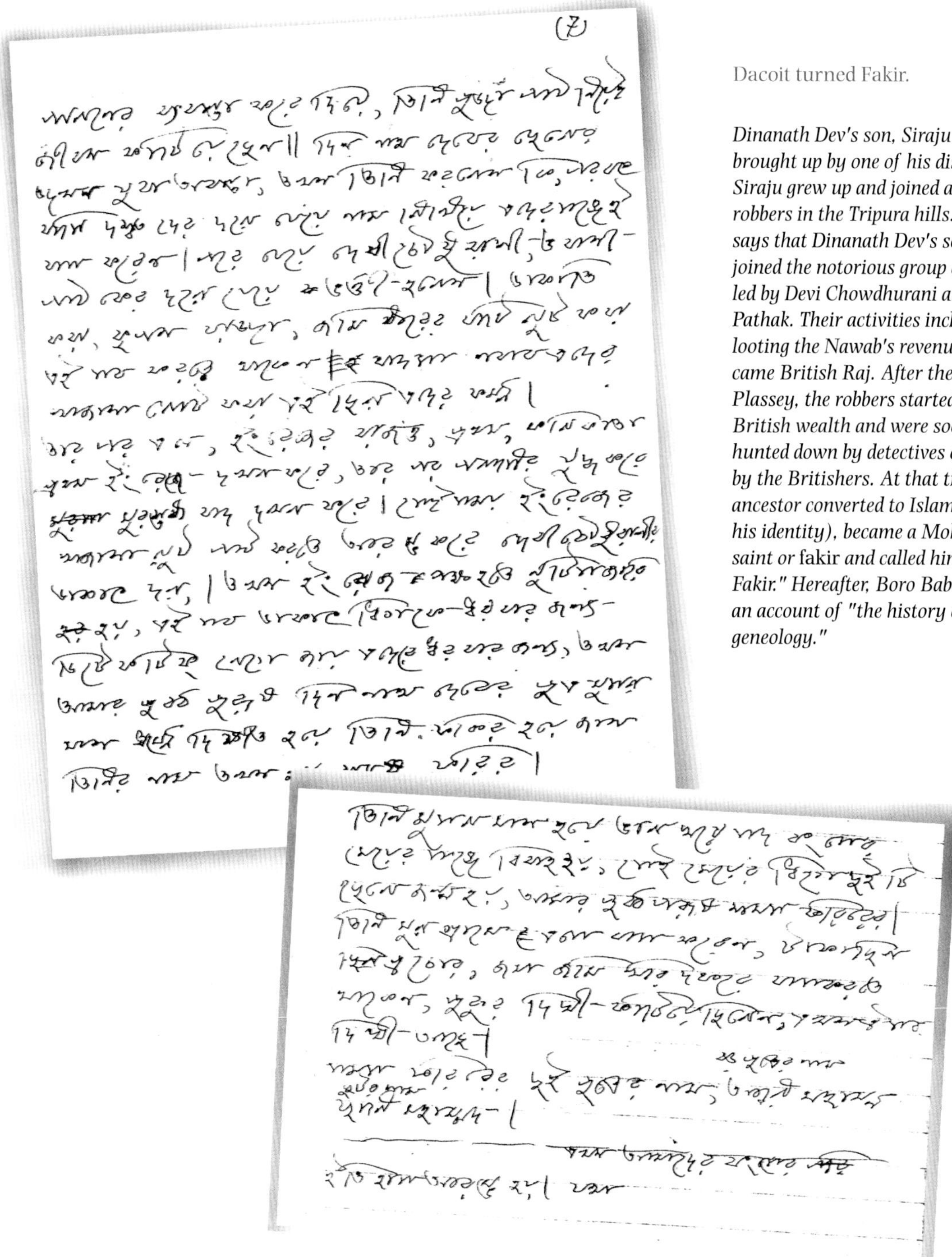

Dacoit turned Fakir.

Dinanath Dev's son, Siraju was brought up by one of his disciples. Siraju grew up and joined a gang of robbers in the Tripura hills. Boro Baba says that Dinanath Dev's son "later joined the notorious group of robbers led by Devi Chowdhurani and Bhabani Pathak. Their activities included looting the Nawab's revenue. Then came British Raj. After the Battle of Plassey, the robbers started targetting British wealth and were soon being hunted down by detectives employed by the Britishers. At that time, my ancestor converted to Islam (to change his identity), became a Mohammedan saint or fakir *and called himself Sams Fakir." Hereafter, Boro Baba gives us an account of "the history of (his) geneology."*

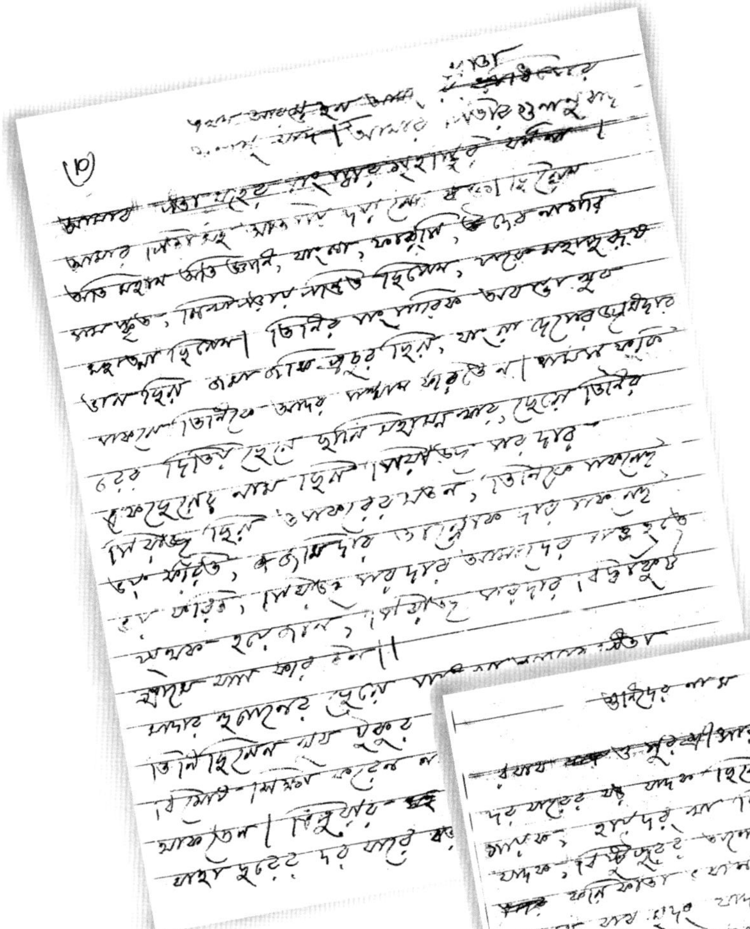

'The Description of my Grandfather'

"My grandfather, Madar Khan, was a kind-hearted simple man. He knew many languages - Bengali, Devnagri, Sanskrit and Persian. He was quite well off with lots of land. The *zamindars* (landlords) of Bangladesh used to respect him."

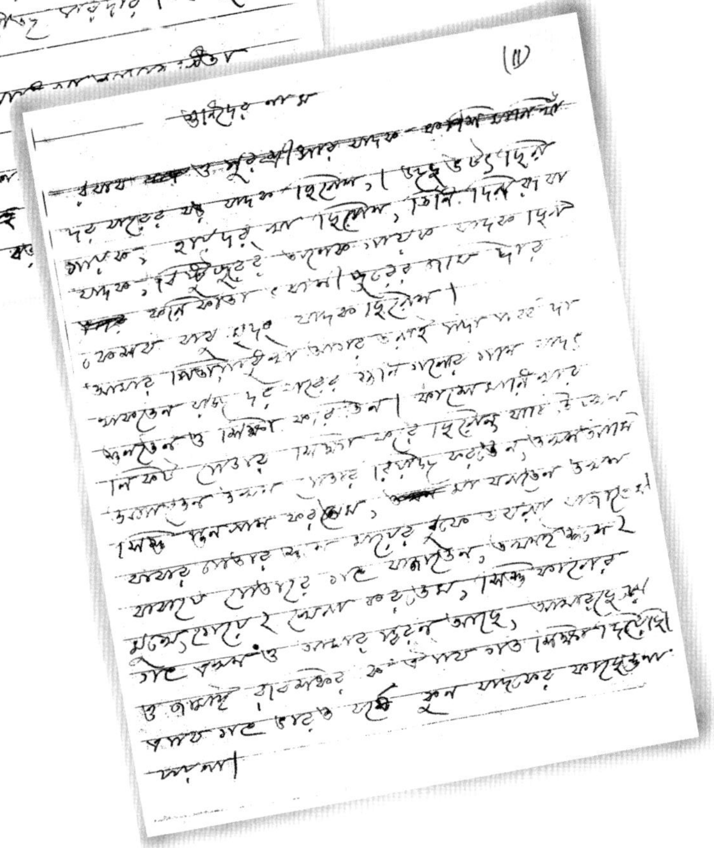

'Talented Persons.'

In this section, Boro Baba tells us of noted musicians who played in the court of the King of Tripura. "Kasim Ali Khan, who played the rabab *and* surshringar, *was the main musician. Jadu Bhatt was the singer, Hyder Khan used to play the* dilruba. *Zamindar Keshav Babu of Kashipore, Kolkata used to play the* mridangam. *My father Sadhu Khan always stayed in the Raj Darbar (royal court) and listened to the music of these talented persons."*

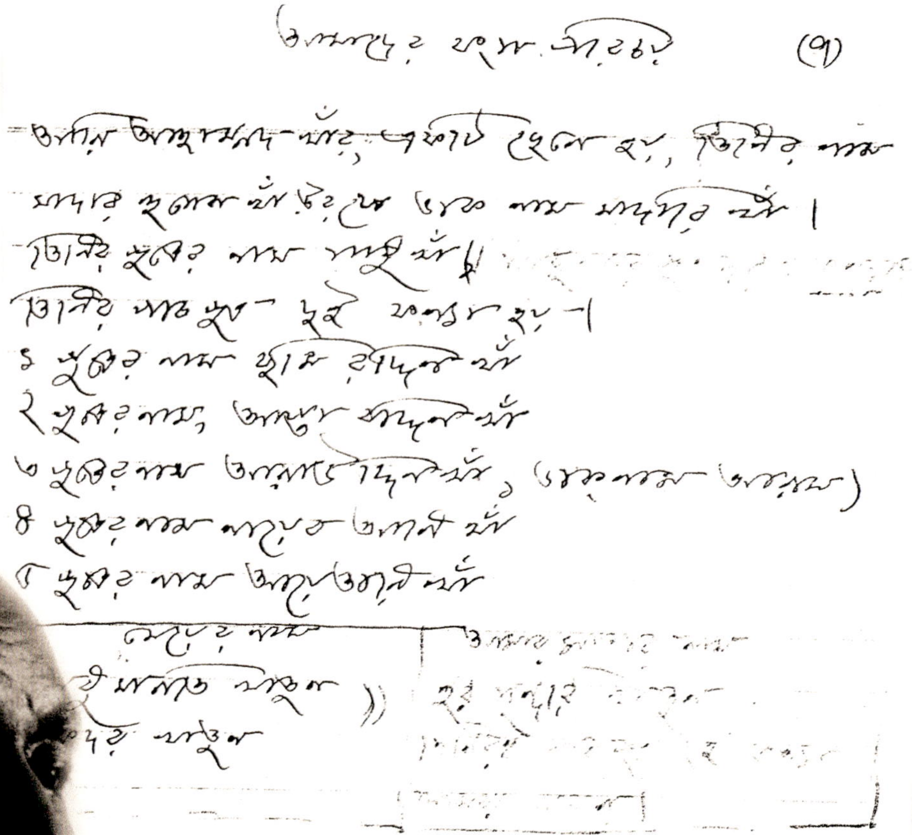

Family History (in Boro Baba's words)

Now, I will outline my family tree: Ali Mohammed Khan had one son who was called Madar Hussain Khan, alias Madar Khan. His son, my father, was Sadhu Khan. Sadhu Khan and his wife Harasundari Devi had five sons and two daughters.

Sons:

1. Samiruddin Khan
2. Aftabuddin Khan
3. Alauddin Khan alias Alam
4. Nayeb Ali Khan
5. Ayet Ali Khan

Daughters:

1. Madhumalati Khatun
2. Kadar Khatun

Family Tree

- DINANATH DEV SHARMA
  - SIRAJU alias SAMS FAKIR (Embraced Islam)
    - Ali Mohammed
      - Madar Hussain Khan alias Madar Khan
        - Sabdar Hussain Khan alias Sadhu Khan *(Wife – Harasundari Devi)*
          - Madhumalati Khatun
          - Samiruddin Khan
          - Aftabuddin Khan
          - Alauddin Khan *(Wife – Madina Begum)*
            - Sarija Begum alias Sarojini
            - Jahanara
            - Ali Akbar Khan *(Wife – Zubeda Khan)*
              - Aashish Khan
              - Dhyanesh Khan *(Wife – Ayesha Khan)*
                - Sahana Gupta née Khan
                - Shiraz Ali Khan
              - Ameena Perera
              - Pranesh Khan
              - Amaresh Khan
            - Roshanara alias Annapurna
          - Nayeb Ali Khan
          - Ayet Ali Khan
          - Kadar Khatun
    - Chhali Mohammed

Boro Baba in Maihar.

Origins

Boro Baba was born in Shibpur village in Tripura, then part of undivided India (now in Bangladesh) and the place where all our forefathers lived. They were, as he notes in his autobiography, Hindus by birth. Baba's ancestors converted to Islam five generations ago. My attempts to unravel the family tree took me up to Dinanath Dev Sharma, about seven generations before us.

Back to Words

Dinanath Dev Sharma was a spiritual man. He had one son, Siraju, after giving birth to whom, his wife passed away. Dinanath managed to bring up his son in the face of many difficulties. But before the child was about eight years old, he decided to renounce worldly life and follow the path of God. He left the young boy in the care of a disciple and set forth to immerse himself in meditation.

Dinanath went on to become a renowned saint and a learned man. He spent the rest of his life at Santayl Parbat, Tripura and had a large following. Maharaja Krishna Kishore Manikya Bahadur ruled over Tripura during the epoch. Dinanath lived the rest of his life in a Kali temple and cut himself from all worldly ties.

Siraju grew up and joined the likes of Devi Chowdhrani, in her fight against social injustice. Although born an aristocrat, Devi Chowdhrani was a bandit hiding in the hills of Tripura, rebelling against the inequitable distribution of wealth. The gang plundered the treasures of the rich; even daring to challenge nawabs; and distributed the wealth among the poor.

After converting to Islam and changing his name to Sams Fakir, to escape arrest, he married a Muslim girl. He had two sons, Ali Mohammed and Chhali Mohammed, and eventually settled down in Moolgram, Bangladesh.

Ali Mohammed Khan had one son, Madar Hussain Khan, alias Madar Khan. Madar Khan was a man of immense knowledge and kindness. He lived in Vidyakut village and was financially sound, with some landholding. The villagers held him in high esteem but he was the sort who was unimpressed by the trappings of rank or status.

Madar Khan's son was Sadhu Khan who, with his wife Harasundari Devi, had five sons – Samiruddin Khan, Aftabuddin Khan, Alauddin Khan, fondly called Alam, Nayeb Ali Khan and Ayet Ali Khan – and two daughters, Madhumalati Khatun and Kadar Khatun. Alauddin Khan was born on the auspicious occasion of Durga Ashtami, AD 1869, in the month of October. In his own handwriting, he quotes his date of birth according to the Bengali calendar as 1269/1268, month: *Aswin, Durga Maha Ashtami, tithi: Brahma Moohartha*. Although Sadhu Khan, lived in Shibpur, he travelled frequently to hear musical performances. The court of Tripura's king, Birchandra Manikya Bahadur, housed many renowned musicians of the time. Such was his love for music, that Sadhu Khan would stand for hours in the sun or rain and even hide in the bushes of the palace, in order to listen to music. One day, he was found hiding and hauled up to the palace where Ustad Kasim Sahib confronted him. Sadhu Khan humbly told him that he was a farmer from Shibpur, who loved music and travelled to Tripura just to hear the Ustad playing the *rabab*. The Ustad was touched by his devotion and even went on to teach him. He taught Sadhu Khan the *sitar* though; instead of the *rabab*, as tradition bid him to pass his art on only to his sons. Thus, Sadhu Khan became a disciple of Ustad Kasim Ali Khan, who belonged to the legendary Tansen's musical lineage; resulting in Boro Baba's rich musical inheritance.

Boro Baba's manuscript indicates that his fascination for music dates back to his infancy: 'Testimony to my passion for music comes from what my mother narrated... She said that as an infant I would listen to my father playing the *sitar* and tap on her bosom in rhythm with the music... I would hum the *gats* which my father played.'

Boro Baba writes about the effect that melody had on his young mind: 'I still remember those *gats* and hymns. I have

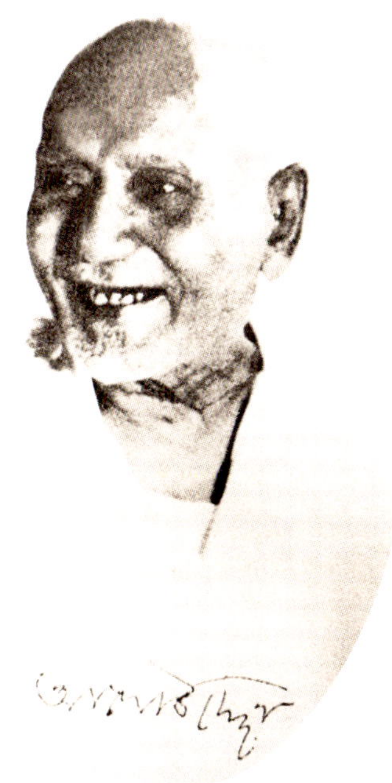

Baba Alauddin Khan.

A rare picture autographed by Boro Baba himself.

taught the same hymns to my son Ali Akbar and son-in-law Ravi Shankar. These pieces of music are not available with any other Indian musician.'

Boro Baba's elder brother, Aftabuddin Khan learned to play the *tabla*, as their father Sadhu Khan had progressed in his *sitar* practise and now felt the need for *tabla* accompaniment. Aftabuddin practised with the *tabla* maestro, Ram Kanai Sil, whose elder brother, Ramdhan Sil, a violinist, taught violin and vocals. By the age of four or five, Boro Baba had learned the *thekas* practised by the tabla maestros and would attempt them on his own.

The Urge to Learn

Boro Baba considers his life to have started at the age of seven, when he realized his passion for music. It was from this age that he began to dedicate every moment of his life to music.

Shibpur, where Boro Baba was raised, had a famous Shiva temple, where morning and evening prayers (*puja* and *aradhana*) were conducted daily. On his way to school, Boro Baba would pass by the temple and stop to watch the prayers. Sadhus from various regions and places assembled there to conduct prayers. They would sing bhajans and play the *sitar*. The sound of music mesmerized Boro Baba and he would forget to attend school.

Boro Baba describes his hunger for music as it developed:

'Gradually, I got habituated to this routine. I woke up early in the morning and went to the temple instead of school. Everyone in the family presumed that I was going to school as I carried my books along and nobody bothered to keep an eye on me. This passion for music gradually compelled me into continued absence from school and I repeatedly turned up at the temple, eager to listen to the sadhus' songs and music. In the evening, when other children returned from school, I too came back with them.'

It wasn't long before his teachers brought the matter of his continual absence to the notice of his parents. Sure enough, he had to bear the brunt of their anger. He was beaten, tied to a bamboo tree and punished in several other ways. But it was too late! By then, Boro Baba's attachment to music had become fiercely strong. At such a young age, he had already decided that he was not going to school any more and would only learn music.

Boro Baba playing truant at his village school, greatly annoyed his *dada* (elder brother), Aftabuddin Khan. Boro Baba fondly recalls the lessons of life he learnt from him; 'Dada had two major shortcomings: a quick temper and an addiction to tobacco. I would arrange for his tobacco behind our house secretly. However, if he did not receive it on time, he exercised his anger on me and beat me up. In contrast, the day he got the tobacco on time, he bestowed his love and affection on me. He would offer me the snout of the hookah and ask me to try it as well. This is how I got addicted. He said that until I smoked tobacco, I would not feel like a man in this world and under its influence, I would experience the essence of a real human being. I am thankful to Dada for teaching me this lesson.'

This child's love for music, was greater than any familial tie. Boro Baba had heard his father saying that there were renowned musicians in the West and Western classical music was the perfect model for a true music lover to imbibe. He claimed that serious studies of music were meant to be pursued in the West. His father would often refer to his Ustad, Kasim Ali Khan 'Rababi', who according to him, was incomparable to other Indian musicians. These opinions instinctively inspired Boro Baba and he decided that if required, he would go abroad to learn music. There arose a need within him to leave the house and start off on his journey without further delay. The young boy also realized that practicality would pay off and started to look out for opportunities.

Around this time, Boro Baba's mother fell sick and became very weak. Her illness, however, turned out to be a blessing in disguise for him. He had to sleep beside her at night to be at hand in case she required any help. One day, he saw a bundle of keys tied to her saree's *pallu*, 'Now is the time!' he told himself. He picked up the keys

Boro Baba's elder brother, Fakir Aftabuddin Khan, playing a *dotara*.

It is said that he could even charm snakes with his music.

FACING PAGE:

Members of Boro Baba's family.

Top: *Boro Baba's parents, Sadhu Khan and Harasundari Devi.* Bottom: *Baro Baba's eldest brother, Samiruddin Khan.*

and opening the boxes lying in the room, gathered the few rupees he found there and bundled them up along with all his clothes in an old saree. Then, Boro Baba says, 'I touched my mother's feet with my head, offering her *pranam*, and left the house.'

It was midnight and this boy, just eight years old, had left home in search of music in the world. He walked eight miles towards Maniknagar station, reached at dawn and boarded a steamer going to Narayanganj. Naive to legalities, Boro Baba travelled without tickets. From Narayanganj, he boarded another steamer going to Goyanand, and there he caught a train to the Sealdah station, Calcutta.

Boro Baba sitting near the Maihar river.

He stayed in Maihar while he was a court musician and spent all his free time practising or composing timeless tunes.

The Escape

2

There is only one thing that makes a dream impossible to achieve: the fear of failure.

—Paulo Coelho

Boro Baba always recalled that the first sight of Sealdah station and Calcutta overwhelmed him. Trains, engines, the wide roads, trams being pulled by horses, people – the entire spectacle scared him.

In his manuscript he writes, 'As I walked, I looked at the people around me, their clothes. It seemed that they did not belong to our country. I did not have the courage to speak to any of them. I also stared at the tall buildings – two, four, five and even seven-storeyed buildings! They were almost touching the sky. I wandered around, not knowing where to go, and stood in the middle of the road, amazed and confused. People passing by gawked at me as if I was a wild being. Some of them even bullied me. Young boys walking on my right and left pulled my ears. I wanted a way out of the situation and decided not to stand still at a place and gape at buildings.'

Boro Baba, walking further to the west, managed to reach the River Ganga near the Howrah Bridge. He then treated himself to some *dal-puri* from a street shop, got himself a container to fetch water and quenched his thirst with the saline water of the river.

Daylight gave way to twilight and then came the dark evening. He saw electric lights for the first time in his life. He recollects that snatches of the luminous light reflecting over the Ganga made it seem like he was gazing at paradise itself. The lad was tired and sleepy but had no shelter for the night. Finally, making a pillow of his small bundle of clothes, the little boy slept on the steps of the riverbank

FACING PAGE:

Sealdah station c. 1867

This is what the station looked like when Boro Baba reached Calcutta.

– very likely with many others. This meagre bundle also contained his fortune of twelve rupees.

The morning, however, had a rude shock in store for Boro Baba. He woke up to find the bundle missing from beneath his head. It was stolen! The poor boy started to cry in the realization that he had been robbed of his sweetest dream in life.

Here, Boro Baba narrates what followed in his own words: 'Some guards standing nearby inquired after the cause of my grief. I told them how my money was stolen. They were unsympathetic and called me an idiot for being so careless. I decided to walk along the riverbank where I came across some ash-smeared sadhus preparing *bhang*. One of the sadhus came up to me and asked me what made me so sad. On hearing my pitiful tale, they consoled me, made me take a dip in the holy river and showed me a straight route to follow before bidding me adieu. I realized that I was in the Neemtala cremation ghat. As I walked down I found a crowd of beggars – blind, handicapped, unclean children, men and women – eating food served on a *shaalpaata* leaf. The Brahmin serving food saw me and asked if I wanted to eat too and served me a helping of *dal* and rice. After my appetite was satiated, I was directed to a nearby tap for a drink of water. The Brahmin guessed that I must be an orphan and when I said that I knew no one in Calcutta, guided me to a dispensary across the road, belonging to one Dr. Kedarnath, so that I could rest at the entrance.'

From then on, that entrance became Boro Baba's shelter where he spent dark, long nights, and he survived on the lone meal served to beggars at the ghat. So it went on for some days.

The boy's mornings must have been spent in aimless sightseeing or getting acquainted with the city and its strange people. But when dusk fell, his pent-up grief burst forth. Every night he cried in sheer desperation, thinking of his plight.

One day, a young boy came to the doctor's chamber to buy some medicines. He had seen Boro Baba sitting at the same place everyday and weeping, so he asked him about his whereabouts. His sympathetic expression made Boro Baba reveal his story and how he landed in this plight in his quest for a guru.

Touched by Boro Baba's tale, the boy promised to take him to his mother. He even added that his father, who learnt music from a senior ustad, could help him find a teacher as well.

The next day, he came back and took Boro Baba home. His mother affectionately held Boro Baba's hand and asked him to follow her inside. Boro Baba stopped her, 'But Maaji, I belong to a Muslim family!' The lady nonchalantly said, 'Doesn't matter, my boy, children are not inhibited by religious affiliations.' She lovingly took him inside and served him *puris* and *mohan bhog halwa*.

She wanted to know all about him and Boro Baba, deprived of any care or concern for a long time, opened himself up before her. The lady was so moved that she called upon her husband, Bireswar Rai Babu, and described the child's obsession for music and what he had done for it. Bireswar Babu was amazed to hear it all and exclaimed that he would surely grow up to become a great singer.

Boro Baba recalls: 'Bireswar Babu asked me if I could sing. I said that I had learnt a few songs from the sadhus in my village, and sang '*Shiva Shankar Hara Hara Bam Bam Bholanath*'. Babuji remarked that my voice was melodious and sweet and I could learn very well. He immediately asked me to accompany him to his guru. I paid my earnest respect to Babuji's wife and proceeded with him to *pathure khata* – guruji's residence. I learnt that his guru was Sri Gopal Chandra Bhattacharya and was known as Nulo Gopal. He was given this name because both his hands were very short.'

A view of the then quiet, yet urbanized Calcutta, late nineteenth century.

3 Formal Education Begins

Only the curious will learn and only the resolute overcome the obstacles to learning.

—Eugene S Wilson

Nulo Gopal was the court musician of the then Raja of Calcutta, Jyotindra Mohan Bhattacharya. Bireswar Babu took Boro Baba to him and told him all he had heard. After a short examination, Guru Nulo Gopal had no hesitation in accepting Boro Baba as his disciple. He said Boro Baba would have to undergo *sur sadhana* for twelve years, after which he would teach him actual songs. Needless to say, Boro Baba was overjoyed and prostrated before the guru in total surrender.

Boro Baba recollects his early learning days: 'Guruji started with *sargam* lessons. He had a disciple called Gangaram Thakur who also cooked for him. Gangaram taught me the *sargam*, *palta* and *alankar*. I had to get up at 2 am and practise these patterns with my guru Nulo Gopal up to 5 am I was happy and enthusiastic to perform this rigorous *sadhana*. Guruji was also pleased with my attitude.' Eager to learn all musical intricacies, he practised playing the *tanpura* with his right hand, the *bayan* (*tabla*) with his left, marking the *tala* with his left foot and recording *matras* with his right.

Through all this, the young Boro Baba survived on just a single meal a day – the free food offered to the beggars at noon. His dinner was a few sips of the salty water of the Ganga. But such was his

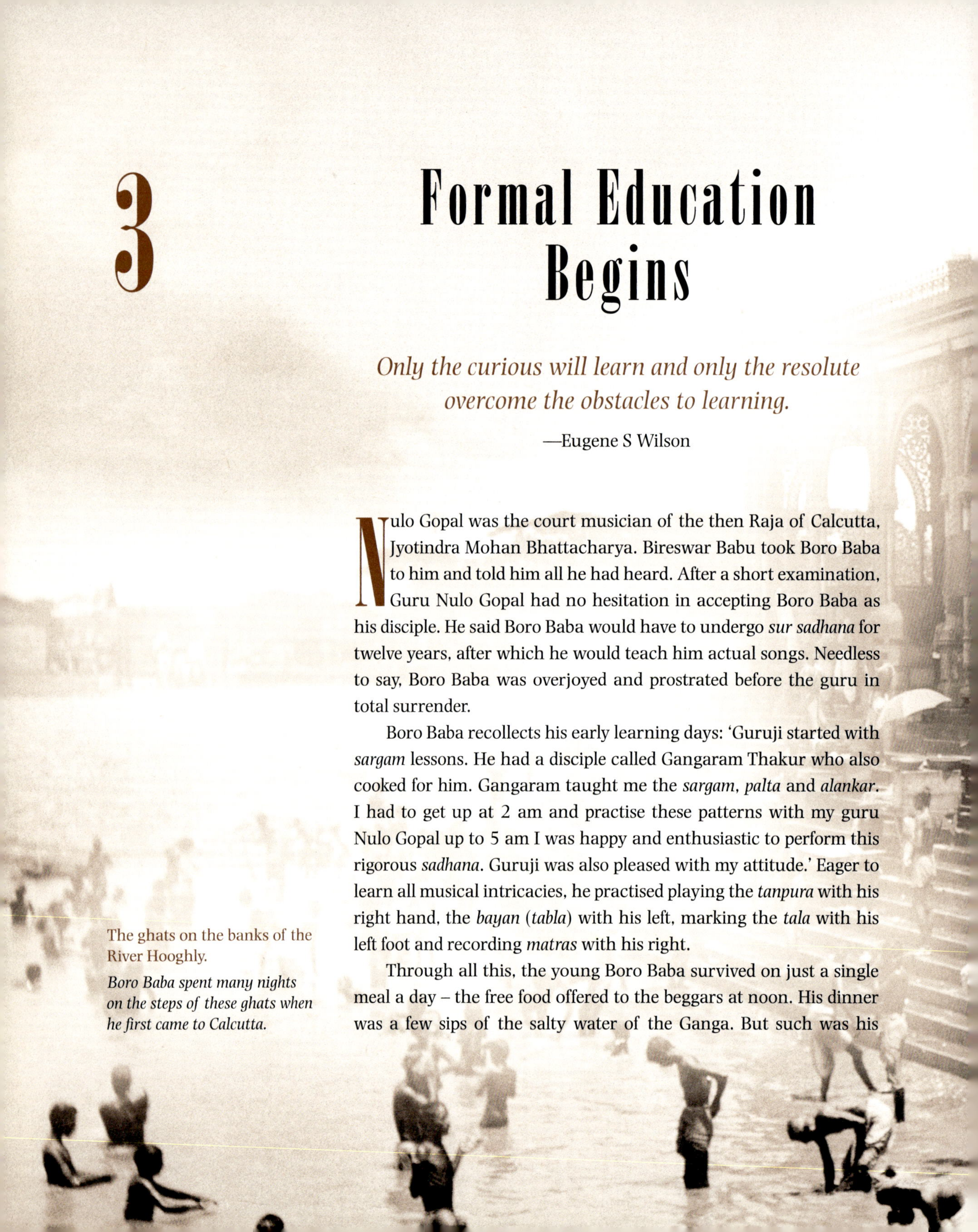

The ghats on the banks of the River Hooghly.

Boro Baba spent many nights on the steps of these ghats when he first came to Calcutta.

devotion to his craft that he never revealed a word of his suffering to his guru or cursed his luck.

Only when Guruji casually enquired about his food did he reveal the truth. Shocked and probably a little embarrassed, Nulo Gopal immediately arranged for his meals at the residence of Kiran Babu – one of Jyotindra Mohan Bhattacharya's brothers.

Boro Baba continued *sur sadhana* with single-minded dedication and spared not a single thought to home or family. Nulo Gopal was no less than a father figure for Boro Baba. He was an exceptional guru in that he shared all his knowledge with his disciples, and in Baba he had found the perfect recipient of his musical heritage.

After about eight years of living in Calcutta and being Nulo Gopal's disciple, Boro Baba received an unexpected visit. It was 1878 and he was now about sixteen years of age. One day, he was surprised to see his elder brother Aftabuddin Khan along with his father-in-law, Mohammed Miya, standing in Guruji's house. They had come looking for him.

The village zamindar's sons were studying in a Calcutta college and had reported seeing Boro Baba to his relatives. Boro Baba's family knew that classical music was practised in places like Bhawanipur and guessed that he must be somewhere there. After conducting some more enquiries, they discovered that he was sheltered by Jyotindra Mohan Bhattacharya's court musician. Delighted to find the missing boy at last, they told Nulo Gopal about his mother's agony and tears and how they all missed him. Of course, they wanted to take him home with them. Said Nulo Gopal, 'Yes, I can understand. I shouldn't mind your taking him home. But the boy is doing well in his *sadhana* and making excellent progress. If you disturb him now, I'm afraid he could be in for a major loss in his life.'

The two men discussed the matter with Guruji, and finally managed permission for a short period of leave with a promise to send Boro Baba back within a month.

An Eventful Month

4

Only through experience of trial and suffering can the soul be strengthened, ambition inspired, and success achieved.

—Helen Keller

Back in the village, everyone was delighted to have their Alauddin back amidst them, but the family's worry was how to keep him back. They finally decided that getting him married was the best option, but kept their plan a secret for the time being.

Boro Baba's bride, in fact, had been chosen long ago. Her name was Madan Manjari and she was the youngest daughter of Basir Khan of Raipur village, and the sister of one of Aftabuddin's pupils. At the time of the decision, Boro Baba was seven years old while the girl in question had just been born. Now, nine years later, Boro Baba's elder brothers and sisters went to Madan Manjari's house, renewed the proposal and settled the wedding date without giving a hint to Boro Baba as they feared he would oppose the idea and put up a fight.

A few days later, Aftabuddin told his brother that they would depart for Calcutta so that he could renew his pursuit of music. The boy was visibly happy and relieved. On the way, they halted at Raipur, where Boro Baba was treated royally, showered with love and affection and served food fit for kings. He must have been intrigued and even felt restive! After four or five days, Aftabuddin broke the news to his brother. He explained that his marriage with Madan Manjari was an unbreakable commitment for all of them, especially for Boro Baba, as this was a pledge their father had made to his friend, Basir Khan.

FACING PAGE:

Alauddin Khan and Madan Manjari.

The nawab of melody with his begum.

Expectably, Boro Baba was upset and unwilling to be tied down, at least for the time being, but the elders insisted that the marriage must be solemnized immediately; only then could he proceed to Calcutta. Finally Boro Baba acquiesced and the wedding took place. Two days after the marriage came the ritual nuptial night, which the newly-weds spend together in the privacy of a room. But what could it have meant to the youngster so engrossed in his own thoughts – what exactly had been going on in his mind is hard for others to guess. Here is an account of what transpired from Boro Baba himself:

'I went inside, saw that my wife was in deep sleep and shut the door. I saw all the jewellery on her – she wore a necklace, a *bajubandh* and other items. I took them off very quietly. There were also some other pieces of jewellery, as well as cash gifted to us, lying in the room. I wrapped them all up in a piece of cloth, latched the door and silently left the house.' It was a bizarre action, but then Boro Baba had always been a maverick.

Without wasting any time, Boro Baba rushed to the nearby Narsindi village to board the steamer bound for Narayanganj. There, he boarded the train to Calcutta and fled to his guru's residence – only to find an empty house with locked doors. He then made his way to Raja Jyotindra Mohan's house where a shocking truth was revealed to him – Nulo Gopal was no more! He had suddenly developed high fever and passed away. Since he had no heir, the government had taken over all his property. This was a dramatic as well as poignant moment for Boro Baba. What was supposed to be just a pause in his journey with the revered guru, had turned out to be a final parting. The guilt of not being with his guru during his last moments tormented him as did disturbing visions of the uncertain future. Boro Baba reminisces about this time:

'The Almighty alone knows what my state of mind then was. I felt that my world had collapsed and the sky had fallen upon me.'

Boro Baba and Boro Ma many years after their marriage.

A rare picture of Boro Baba and Boro Ma looking happy on their wedding anniversary.

The Raja's brother and Boro Baba's host, Kiran, discussed with him his plans for the future. Dejected and depressed, Boro Baba replied that he would give up vocal training and pursue instrumental music. Kiran, too, expressed his wholehearted approval for this idea.

This decision led to the need of finding a new teacher. Kiran thought it over and suggested that Habu (or Amrit Lal) Dutta of Shimla, based in Calcutta, would be an ideal teacher. Dutta was Swami Vivekananda's cousin and the music director of the Star Theatre. He was an expert in many instruments, a considerate man and even taught free of cost.

Time-tested togetherness.

Baro Baba with Boro Ma in Madina Bhawan.

Mastering Instruments

5

Everyone has talent. What is rare is the courage to follow the talent to the dark place where it leads.

—Erica Jong

Boro Baba searched for Habu Babu's place, met him and gave him a candid overview of his past. Habu Dutta, pleased with his talent as well as frankness, accepted him as a disciple and offered to teach him the violin and cornet. With the money that he had carried from home, Boro Baba bought the two instruments.

In this manner, his instrumental lessons under the tutelage of Habu Dutta started. The initial training period was devoted to the *swargam*, through which he was made aware of finer points of notes and *swar*. The instruction went on for seven years, at the end of which he could play 360 *paltas*. Under his new teacher, Boro Baba became proficient in various indigenous as well as foreign musical instruments, like the *sitar*, flute, piccolo, mandolin and banjo under his new teacher. Habu Dutta was quick to recognize the genius in Boro Baba and remarked that he would be widely acknowledged and feted as such someday.

In the meantime, instead of being satisfied and complacent, Boro Baba became frantic to master every instrument that he could lay his hands on and eagerly looked for opportunities to further his musical knowledge. Even while learning music from Nulo Gopal, he had started *mridangam* lessons from a guru named Nanda Babu.

He learnt the violin in the notation of Western music from Mr Lobo, a Goanese bandmaster at Eden Gardens, and the clarinet

FACING PAGE:

Boro Baba trying out his skills on the *rabab* (above) and *sarode* (below).

Although Boro Baba was left-handed, he was remarkably skilled at playing innumerable instruments, many of which were his own inventions.

Master of Melody.

A rare picture of Boro Baba with the pakhawaj. *He was a master of many instruments which he spent a lifetime in learning.*

Boro Baba playing the *surshringar*.

The surshringar *is a beautiful instrument which is almost extinct today. Its neck, with a metal fingerboard, resembles the* sarode. *It was used as a solo instrument in the nineteenth and the twentieth centuries.*

and cornet from another Western teacher in Darjipara, Calcutta. He learnt the Indian style of the violin from Amar Das, a prominent musician of the time. He became conversant with complicated instruments like the *sanai, naquara, tiquara* and *jagajhampa* under the able guidance of Hazari Ustad, and prevailed upon Nanda Babu to teach him percussion instruments such as the *pakhawaj, mridangam* and *tabla*.

However, to find the right guru and persuade him to teach, was not always easy. This is illustrated by the manner in which Boro Baba won over the Lobos.

The Lobos lived in Bowbazar, Calcutta and in those days Boro Baba was staying in an optics house behind their house. Both of them were accomplished artists – Mr. Lobo played the violin and his wife played the piano. Boro Baba records in his memoirs that their *jugalbandi* was so melodious, it drove him out of his mind with longing and desperation. He could no longer contain his urge to be accepted by them for tutelage. He waited in front of their house nearly everyday but never got to see Mr. Lobo. He would greet Mrs. Lobo but dared not ask her anything.

Boro Baba playing the violin.

Boro Baba took lessons in European classical violin and popularized the instrument by playing it in an Indian style.

One day, on his way for violin lessons, he saw the Lobos sitting outside their house. He approached and saluted them. Mrs. Lobo enquired from whom he had been learning the violin and asked him to play a bit. Instantly, Boro Baba showcased his talent playing the *sargam* and the *palta* to the best of his ability. 'Beautiful! You can play well,' remarked the lady. Thus encouraged, Boro Baba pleaded with Mr. Lobo to accept him as a student. Lobo, however, flared up and abused him, calling Boro Baba 'a bloody pig', and even hitting him. What incensed Lobo so much is not clear. Probably, he could not tolerate the perceived audacity of an unsophisticated, rustic and poor young man. However, even that did not put off Boro Baba who looked to a more sympathetic

Mrs. Lobo for succour and got it too! About this incident he says, 'Later, Memsaheb (Mrs. Lobo) caught hold of me and advised me to come to her house the next day at 1 pm, when the Saheb left for office and wouldn't object to my learning at that time (from her).'

Tryst with Theatre

Learning to master so many musical instruments and forms simultaneously from different teachers was, undoubtedly, a very rewarding experience for Boro Baba in the prime of his youth. Being able to afford it, however, was another matter. Having to pay so many teachers, he almost ran out of money, and confided in Habu Dutta about this. He could already play diverse instruments like the violin, cornet, clarinet, *shehnai*, flute, *tabla*, *mridangam* and *dholak*, it was not very difficult for such a proficient young man to obtain a job as a musician. Habu Dutta took him to Girish Chandra Ghosh, a leading theatre personality, and got him a job in his troupe.

Girish Ghosh (later immortalized by his association with Sri Ramakrishna Paramahamsa as an embodiment of devotion and faith) was a legendary figure of the Bengali theatre. He was an outstanding playwright, actor, poet, producer, manager and teacher all rolled into one, and reigned over the theatre for four decades. He catered to middle-class emotions, sentiments and interests through his farces, burlesques, musicals and fantasies. He composed social dramas, religious and quasi-historical plays and tapped the pulse of the audience with his comic interludes as well as patriotic fervour.

The theatre where Boro Baba came to work was called the Minerva Theatre and its proprietor was Girish Ghosh himself. Impressed by Boro Baba's extensive repertoire, Ghosh handed over the complete responsibility of the musical parts in his plays to the young man. One day, during rehearsals, he listened to the many instruments that Boro Baba played and was impressed. Boro Baba was the only Muslim in the theatre but Ghosh had no communal biases. However, to conceal his true identity for fear of discrimination from others, Ghosh gave him the pseudonym of Prasanna Kumar Biswas and addressed him as such. Boro Baba's financial condition started to look up and for the first time in years, food and shelter were no longer a problem. As a bonus, during the next three years, he learnt many popular songs from the theatre and improved his instrumental proficiency greatly.

Girish Chandra Ghosh, a noted poet, playwright, and actor, was one of Bengal's greatest dramatists.

Considered the father of Bengali drama, he ran his own theatre company in Calcutta.

Despite this, however, Boro Baba was never comfortable with theatre life. He despised the company of drunkards and people of dubious character, and always lived in fear. Finally, when it became unbearable for him to continue, he went to his employer and laid bare his concerns. Girish Ghosh was very understanding and said that Boro Baba was indeed playing with fire in the theatre. Without trying to constrain Boro Baba in any way, he said that in such circumstances, it was better for Boro Baba to go ahead and dedicate his life to music and sent him off with his best wishes.

Back to Learning

6

To have striven, to have made the effort,
to have been true to certain ideals –
this alone is worth the struggle.

—William Penn

Boro Baba had heard of the Durga Puja celebrations conducted by the Muktagacha zamindars in the Moymon Singh district in present-day Bangladesh, where reputed musicians and ustads often performed. Now that he had learnt music for many years and mastered various instruments, Boro Baba felt he, too, could rightfully perform there and please the audience.

This was possibly one of the first instances where Boro Baba allowed his pride to cloud his judgement. He had begun to consider himself a very accomplished musician. He believed that if he sang all that he had learnt in the theatre, 'it would stir up a storm among the audience.' However, the reality was different. The young man, barely twenty-five, had seen little of the world and didn't realize that he had yet to prove himself among the many legends who ruled over the world of music. His vanity was soon to be crushed. Later he laments, 'I had this devil of a pride in me.'

With this inflated view of his own talent, he reached the durbar of Raja Jagat Kishore Acharya. With a violin, cornet and *shehnai* in his bag, he approached Jagat Kishore, gave a brief introduction of himself and said boastfully that he was an ustad, having learnt music for over fifteen years and proficient in many instruments; he had come to the durbar in order to showcase his art. Jagat Kishore gave him a look, nodded smilingly and said, 'Sure, why not! We will definitely listen to you,' and instructed a courtier to arrange a place

FACING PAGE:

Boro Baba reading the *Rahasya Patrika*, a popular Bengali journal of the time.

He loved reading and was especially fond of detective fiction.

FACING PAGE:
Boro Baba playing the *sarode*.

for him to stay. As he left, the ruler gestured to the courtier, indicating that Boro Baba was crazy. Though Boro Baba saw the exchange, he ignored what it apparently meant. He was told to present himself at the court at 8 am the next day.

When Boro Baba arrived with his cornet and violin at the scheduled time, the court was filled with an audience waiting in silence – presumably to hear the new ustad. But there was another artist about to start the recital. A handsome young man, with a close beard and sporting an ornate cap, was tuning the *sarode*, accompanied by a *tanpura* player. As Boro Baba watched, he was amazed by the manner in which he tuned his instruments. There was something extraordinary about the way he handled the strings. And what he played thereafter, left Boro Baba awestruck! He had never heard such a *raga* in his entire musical journey. Later, he came to know that it was *Raga Darbari Todi*. Boro Baba describes his experience thus:

'When he started his recital, and moved from note *ni* to *sa*, I was startled. As he started the *alaap*, I just could not control my tears, and eventually began to cry. He went on to the *taan*, and it churned my innards. I burst out crying, even as the audience enjoyed the music quietly. Ustadji saw me and started playing strange melodies and notes that were full of emotions and sensation. Tears rolled down from my eyes incessantly. I had never heard such a melodious and powerful recital of the *sarode*. Ustadji kept on playing spontaneously till 1 pm As soon as he put down the *sarode*, I ran to him and put my head on his feet.' This phenomenal performer was none other than Ahmed Ali Khan.

Boro Baba was introduced by Jagat Kishore to the ustad. Boro Baba then pleaded with Ustadji, 'It is by Jagajjanani Ma's grace that I have found you. She has showed me the ideal guru. I implore you to accept me as a disciple.' Seeing his sincerity, Ustadji responded positively. The audience, including Jagat Kishore and other learned musicians too, chorused approvingly. At this sensational moment, Raja Jagat Kishore ordered his attendants to provide all the items required for the formal acceptance ceremony of a disciple. Accordingly, Ustad

Ahmed Ali Khan tied the *nara*, thread, around Boro Baba's wrist and the Raja presented Boro Baba with a *sarode*.

For the next three years, Boro Baba lived with Ahmed Ali Khan, serving him and learning the *sarode*.

A Sweet and Sour Relationship

Ahmed Ali Khan was employed as a *sarode* player by Duli Chand, a rich Marwari who lived in Ghugudanga, Calcutta. Other talented artists including a female singer, a *sarangi* accompanist by the name of Badal Khan, and a *thumri* singer called Maijuddin Khan were also sheltered by Duli Chand.

After his induction as a disciple, it was part of Boro Baba's responsibility to take care of all the household chores. He did everything a servant would be expected to – cooking, cleaning the house and the toilet, arranging for tobacco puffs, shopping and also massaging his master's feet before the latter went to sleep. Ustadji had taught Boro Baba how to prepare a number of Hindustani delicacies such as *pulao*, *korma*, *rotis*, *paranthas*, *shammi* and *seekh kababs* and *zarda*. If there were any guests visiting the house, Boro Baba had to cook for them as well. Although all these tasks were a lot for a single person to handle, Boro Baba never complained.

Ahmed Ali Khan occasionally went for *mujras* (concerts) in Calcutta, where Boro Baba accompanied him on the tabla and sometimes on the *mridangam*. Occasionally, he was even allowed to give *sath* (company) on the violin, a performance that was much appreciated by the audience. In fact, there were times when the sound of his violin was considered superior to Ahmed Ali Khan's *sarode*, and Boro Baba stole the show. These concerts were an indication of Boro Baba's musical genius.

Ahmed Ali Khan, however, did not mind Boro Baba's little successes and conducted himself with grace. In fact, he shared the income from the *mujras* equally with Boro Baba, and even left all his earnings in his disciple's care.

The initial days of Boro Baba's training were spent in familiarizing himself with the basic techniques of *sarode* playing. After breakfast and tea had been prepared for his guru in the mornings, he would start on lunch. Before lunch was ready, he would steal some time for *sarode* practise. After Ustadji came home in the afternoon, ate and rested, Boro Baba again practised every nuance his guru had taught him, but behind closed doors.

Again at 4 pm, Boro Baba would prepare tea and snacks for his guru and start his *riyaz*. Ustadji, if he wished, sometimes called Boro Baba and gave him lessons on *gat* and *tura*. Boro Baba would read his evening *namaz* and again get back to his music.

Gradually, his instincts developed to such an extent that he could immediately pick up whatever Ustadji played in the *mujras*, and on their return home, he practised the same. He learnt all the *ragas* and intricacies of styles like the *lori*, the *lar* and the *gat* just by listening to his guru perform. As he improved and trained in *gatkari*, *vilambit gat* and *dhrut gat*, he soon became skilled enough to play with Ustadji at an equal pace in public concerts. Boro Baba had still not been taught the *alaap*, but his natural genius enabled him to master it by himself.

Boro Baba absorbed in *riyaz* at his residence in Maihar.

When he was finally able to render the *vilambit gat* (slow tempo), the *dhrut gat* (fast tempo, marks the climax of the performance) and the *jhala (*a fast section coming at the end of the *alaap*) flawlessly, Boro Baba felt humbled by a feeling of great satisfaction and contentment. He thanked God profusely for enabling him to achieve such landmarks in music. 'Tears of joy rolled down as I thanked the Almighty for his kindness in fulfilling my wishes,' he writes.

At the same time, he was aware of the price he had paid for it – the injustice he had meted to his loved ones. Confesses Boro Baba, 'I always had the guilt of having hurt my parents and wife, and asked for forgiveness from God.'

However, Boro Baba's journey on the path of learning was not without the obvious peril – that of displeasing his guru. His natural exuberance and passion for music was taking precedence over propriety. Boro Baba was aware of this risk, for he had been practising a number of untaught lessons without his guru's knowledge. The inevitable happened one day. Ahmed Ali Khan was visiting the city and Boro Baba, being home alone, was practising *Raga Darbari Todi*, replicating the style and approach of the Ustad, trying to bring out every nuance in the composition just like the maestro. He was so absorbed in the music that he didn't hear Ustadji return. As he stood listening to it silently, Ustadji was stunned and felt let down. When the playing stopped, there was a knock on the door. Boro Baba opened the door to find his guru glaring at him with a stern face.

'So, who taught you all this? And to play in this method? Tell me the truth!' demanded Ustadji.

Though shaken, Boro Baba kept his composure and answered truthfully – that he had learnt all that from Ustadji himself, by listening attentively and repeated practise.

'But you are doing it without my knowledge, and when I'm away! You are copying me, isn't it? You are a thief!' seethed the guru.

Boro Baba tried his best to appease him, recalling their first meeting when Ustadji had played the same *raga*; how heavenly it sounded when he heard it for the first time and Ustadji's instrument

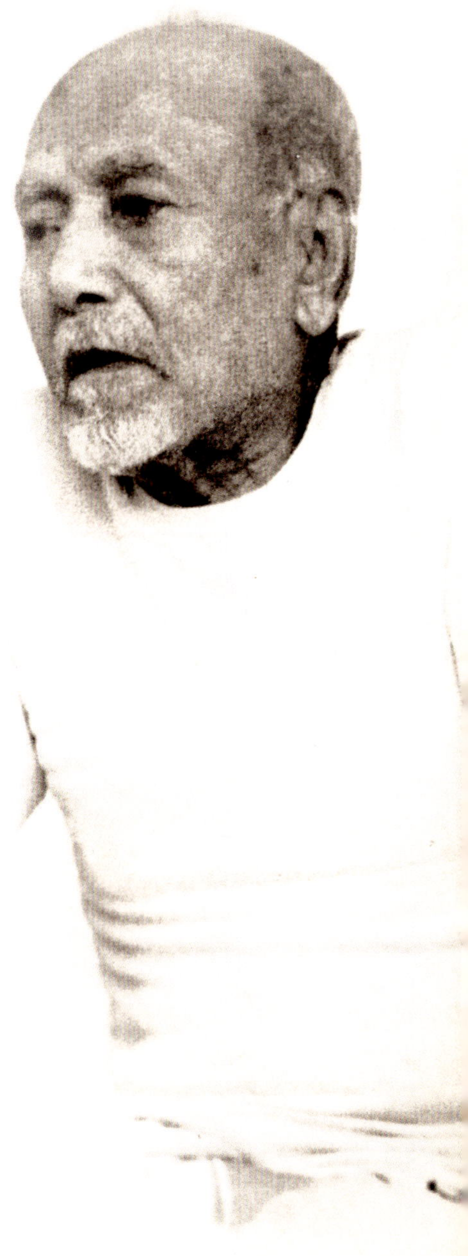

appeared divine. He also described how he was instantly captivated and his ego shattered. Those impressions were still etched in his heart, for which he was eternally grateful to his guru. All his knowledge he verily owed to his guru – whether taught directly or indirectly, Ustadji was the source of it.

Ustadji calmed down a little on hearing Boro Baba's sincere explanation. Then Boro Baba further said that if this action of his was unpardonable, then he would never play the untaught music again, but just play the *alaap* that Ustadji had taught. Though Ahmed Ali Khan did not say anything more, he appeared unconvinced. Much of his goodwill for his disciple appeared to have eroded.

One day, he asked Boro Baba to accompany him to his native village in Rampur, in present-day Uttar Pradesh. The main purpose of this visit was to meet a great ustad named Wazir Khan, the court musician of the ruler, Nawab Bahadur Hamid Ali Khan. Wazir Khan was reputedly unsurpassed by any other musician of his time.

They stayed for a month at the Nawab's house. Ahmed Ali introduced his disciple as being proficient in *sarode* as well as many other instruments. Ustad Wazir Khan said he would like to hear Boro Baba play the *sarode* and the violin. The following day, the sheer perfection of Boro Baba's performance on the violin led the Ustad to exclaim spontaneously, 'Oh, I have never heard such a violin recital before!'

In fact, the Nawab Bahadur was so pleased that he told Ahmed Ali that he wished to hear Boro Baba play the violin again. At the royal personage's request, Boro Baba performed that entire night on the violin, concluding with *Raga Bhairavi*. The Nawab honoured both the guru and the disciple handsomely, rewarding the Ustad with Rs 2,000 and Boro Baba with Rs 5,000 – a princely sum by any standards!

Then, with his master's permission, Boro Baba went to Varanasi and stayed there for three months, giving performances. Having earned over Rs 2,000 there, he returned to Rampur. Ustad Ahmed Ali, who was visiting his parents there and living in their small house, introduced his disciple to them. Boro Baba greeted them respectfully.

In the course of the conversation, Boro Baba told his guru that

FACING PAGE:

Making memorable music.

Boro Baba with his sarode *outside his room.*

he was carrying all the money given to him over a period of time – including those earned by the Ustad in *mujras* and as salary, and offered to hand it over now. It was all in a trunk that he had been carrying from Calcutta.

The Ustad, a little surprised, said that whatever he had earned earlier must have been spent on food and household expenses and there could be no savings. In fact, the servants who served him prior to Boro Baba had always said so, which was why he had never asked Boro Baba for an account. But, Boro Baba was not a servant – he was a disciple managing the money!

Boro Baba then brought the trunk and explained that all the money he had received and saved was in it. Ustadji found many small bundles of notes, which came up to almost Rs 10,000! Boro Baba insisted that every penny was entirely his guru's. Needless to say, the Ustadji and his parents were amazed to see the integrity of this young man. Ustadji's father, Abed Ali Khan, commented that the youth was very honest and was sure to reach great heights in his life. He further remarked that once his son had referred to this disciple as cunning and clever, but he was wrong. When Boro Baba bent to touch the feet of Ustadji's mother, she also blessed him.

Ahmed Ali Khan's immediate worry was what he would do with all the money and what his priorities were. The total amount in his hands was about Rs 15,000. It was decided that they would construct a concrete house. Soon, carts full of bricks, cement and lime started arriving. Boro Baba was asked to unload these materials, and he obliged dutifully. For the next six months, Boro Baba was completely involved in the construction, putting in hard labour. At the end of it, he fell sick and suffered a great deal. He had no money left with him since he had given away all his savings to his master.

In the Clutches of Desperation

In the meantime, Boro Baba had taken up a small house near the Ustadji's home for a rent of eight annas.

Though he lived in that house, he worked and cooked for his teacher and ate his meals there. Since beef was their favourite, Boro Baba had to cook it regularly despite his strong dislike for it, while he himself survived on plain *dal* and *roti*.

Boro Baba started suffering from severe body pain. To alleviate it, he took allopathic medicines, but to no avail. Finally, with a *hakim*'s traditional treatment, he recovered. Despite this, he could not afford a balanced diet which he badly required. The healing process, therefore, was very slow. In spite of his poor health and constant pain, he continued his service at his teacher's house.

After the construction was finally complete, Ustadji went back to Calcutta to resume his work. This ended Boro Baba's apprenticeship under him. Not knowing what to do next, Boro Baba confessed his helplessness to the Ustad's father, Abed Ali Khan, who himself offered to teach him.

Boro Baba started his lessons under him, but it took him nowhere for the old man seemed to have neither the urge nor the talent for the job. Finally, he excused himself saying that there was nothing more he could teach. Boro Baba was saved the trouble of working for that household, but earning his daily bread itself became a problem. He visited many learned musicians in Rampur, but no one was willing to teach free of cost. They expected, on an average, a monthly fee of Rs 100. Boro Baba's misery was only compounded by illness and poverty. He cried in agony and prayed to God to show him a way out of his terrible plight. He started spending most of his time at a nearby mosque, pleading with God to relieve him of this extreme suffering. There were times when he spent the entire day in plaintive prayers.

He ended up eating very irregularly, sometimes surviving for two to three days only on water. When Boro Baba would get to eat once a day after going hungry for a length of time, he felt as if he was feasting on the choicest of food. He spent about two months in this state. In the meantime, he gathered his will power and decided to meet the reputed musician, Ustad Wazir Khan, to seek his help but the guards at the bungalow did not allow him to pass the gateway. Probably, looking at his state, nobody could recognize that he was the artist who, not long ago, had won the praise of Wazir Khan himself. He tried to get an audience with the Ustad everyday for two months but returned disappointed.

At last, out of frustration, Boro Baba got himself some *afeem* (opium), inhaled it and sat inebriated in the mosque premises. Seeing him in that condition, the *maulvi* of the mosque asked him why he was so dejected. When Boro Baba narrated the events that led him to this state, the *maulvi* tried to cheer him up, saying, 'Come on! *Himmate maddata, maddate Khuda* (If you try, God will help you),' and gave him something to eat. Then he discussed a plan with Boro Baba and wrote a detailed note to this effect, addressed to Nawab Bahadur Hamid Ali Khan on his behalf:

'Sir, I am Alauddin from Tripura. I came here six months ago, eager to pursue music. Your durbar boasts of an incredibly learned musician like Ustad Wazir Khan just as the Mughal durbar had the pride of sheltering Mian Tansen. Anxious to learn from Ustadji, I have been visiting his house for the past many months but the guards have not allowed me to meet him. I am greatly disappointed. I request Your Highness to take pity on a poor man and arrange for me to learn music from him. I am already in such despair that, if my ambition is not met, I don't want to live. If you do not intervene, I will have to end my life. This is my last effort and I am carrying *afeem* in my pocket for the purpose. The only reason that I have desisted so far is because committing suicide is considered to be a heinous crime.'

The *maulvi* advised Boro Baba to wait for the opportune moment and hand over the note to the Nawab when he stepped out of his house. Boro Baba agreed and went to the Nawab's house with this poignant appeal nestled in his pocket. But meeting the Nawab was not an easy task. Boro Baba went to his bungalow twice every day – morning and evening – for almost a month and waited at the main entrance, but without luck.

FACING PAGE:

Boro Baba.

Boro Baba would go into a trance and then get back and dazzle the world with splendid tunes.

Ustad Wazir Khan and Others

7

The gem cannot be polished without friction, nor man without trials.

—Confucius

One day, the Nawab was on his way to see a play written by Ustad Wazir Khan. Just as the Nawab's carriage came out, Boro Baba ran directly into its path and stood with his arms spread wide, forcing the carriage to stop. The police arrived to drag him away. Nawab Bahadur Hamid Ali Khan demanded to know the reason for the commotion. A senior police officer reported that a Bengali man had purposely come in the way and caused an obstruction which had forced the vehicle to stop in its tracks. The Nawab, instead of being annoyed, demanded to meet the man who was responsible for this diversion. When brought before the Nawab, Boro Baba handed him the appeal as well as the *afeem* tablets, saluted and stood aside silently. Nawab Bahadur asked his private secretary to read the letter.

When the letter was read out to him, the Nawab was touched by its fervent appeal. He cancelled his theatre programme for the day, ordering his retinue to proceed. He sent his secretary to bring Wazir Khan to Hamid Manzil (named after himself) and took Boro Baba there. On the way, Nawab Bahadur Hamid Ali Khan, himself a very knowledgeable musician and a prime disciple of Ustad Wazir Khan, enquired about Boro Baba's past. Boro Baba gave a brief description of his education, saying that he had done *sur sadhana* under his first guru, Nulo Gopal, for seven years and, after his untimely demise,

FACING PAGE:

Boro Baba posing for a photograph.

Even success and the immense adulation of his fans could never bring Boro Baba to change his simple way of life.

Painting of Mian Tansen, founder of the Senia *gharana*.

This painting is kept in Boro Baba's Maihar residence.

started learning the violin, cornet, clarinet, *shehnai* and *sarode*. The Nawab then asked Boro Baba to bring his instruments to his residence and even arranged for a car for him. Boro Baba returned quickly with the violin and the *sarode*. On the Nawab's orders, Boro Baba demonstrated his knowledge and skill by singing the *sargam*, *palta* and so on. Nawab commented that his education in music had followed the correct path and it would not be a problem to proceed further. Then Boro Baba played the *alaap*, the *jod*, the *jhala* and the *lori* on his *sarode*. The Nawab Bahadur, who had mastered *dhrupad sangeet*, listened appreciatively and praised him effusively. When Boro Baba started playing his violin, the Nawab was very pleased and exclaimed that there was possibly no one in India who could play it as well as Boro Baba.

When Wazir Khan joined him along with the secretary, Nawab Bahadur narrated the morning's events and explained why he could not be present at the theatre. Then, introducing Boro Baba, he said that whatever the young man had learned till then was correct and disciplined and asked Wazir Khan to take him on as a disciple. Ustad Wazir Khan had no hesitation in giving his assent. Immediately, according to the Nawab's wish, arrangements were made for the ritual induction of Boro Baba as a disciple. Wazir Khan tied the *ganda* – the ceremonial sacred thread that is a pledge on the part of a guru to impart to the student all the knowledge that he possesses without holding anything back – around his wrist. Since offering the guru some gold was a mandatory part of the ceremony and Boro Baba did not have any, Hamid Ali Khan offered a *jarao* bangle on the young man's behalf. All other required items including some *ashrafi* (gold coins) were brought on a gold plate and offered to the Ustad. Boro Baba considered himself blessed to be accepted as a disciple of Ustad Wazir Khan. He was also sanctioned lodging near the Ustad's house. Boro Baba, then expressed his desire to learn the *veena*, a claim which the Nawab Bahadur supported, but the Ustad in turn refused, saying that he could teach the *veena* only to his successors and blood relations. On hearing this, Boro Baba replied that he would be more than happy to learn the *sarode*, the *rabab* and the *surshringar* from this eminent teacher.

When the range of his talents became evident, all the court musicians started to hold Boro Baba in high regard. However, with no money in his hand, he struggled to make ends meet. He joined a string band headed by Dule Khan, a renowned *dhrupad* singer and a court musician of the Nawab. Pleased with Boro Baba's violin skills, he offered him a monthly salary of Rs 12 a month, to play the violin in his troupe. It was a meagre amount, but enough to earn two meals a day. He worked for about three hours with the band in the morning. In fact, out of the paltry amount he earned, he started spending Rs 5 as a fee for another teacher he had found – Ustad Mohammed Ali Khan. He was a kind old man, and taught the *dhrupad*, the *dhamar*, the *hori*, the *saadra*, the *tarana* and *gats* in age-old *bandish*. Mohammed Ali Khan and his wife, who were childless, treated him as their own son and showered their love on him. Boro Baba was eternally grateful to Mohammed Ali Khan for everything he had learnt from him.

Tragically, the studentship under Wazir Khan, for which he had craved and which was realized in a truly dramatic fashion, did not materialize as one would have envisaged. Though he accepted Boro Baba as a disciple, Wazir Khan seemed to have almost forgotten him. Boro Baba would wait all morning – from six till ten – at the doorsteps of the Ustad's house but he seldom got a chance to learn from him. So Boro Baba looked out for other teachers and learnt, albeit a trifle stealthily, from them. He would go to Mohammed Hussain Khan for *sarode* lessons and to bandmaster Raja Hussain Khan for *dhrupad*. He also learnt a great deal about *gat* and *tura* in the *sitar* from Ustad Hafiz Khan's brother, Karim Khan. This accumulation of musical knowledge kept Boro Baba somewhat happy and contented. In this manner, he spent about three years of his life in Rampur.

Ustad Wazir Khan.

Boro Baba mastered the Senia gharana *style from Ustad Wazir Khan.*

8

Madan Manjari – The Faithful

Faith is knowledge within the heart,
beyond the reach of proof.
—Kahlil Gibran

Fifteen long years had passed since Boro Baba's marriage to Madan Manjari. The young girl, who was seven when she married, had lived in the care of her parents and three brothers through this long period. The fact that she had reached the prime of her youth and beauty and yet, was forced by circumstances to lead the life of a spinster, deeply disturbed her family. They had been perturbed about her vagabond husband all these years, not sure whether he was alive or dead. Neither possibility would have seemed better than the other! The stigma of widowhood could sap the young girl's life of all vitality forever. But if alive, they feared, he could possibly be worse than dead. If the way he had run away after marriage – with cash and jewellery – was not indication enough, his uncaring absence all these long years itself aroused apprehension. Moreover, with music and theatre personalities in those days being suspect in the matters of morality, chances were, he could have fallen into the company of promiscuous women. So, the family decided to get the girl remarried before it was too late.

Ironically, the only one who was completely opposed to this idea was Madan Manjari herself. One would have expected a young girl in such conditions to be eager to settle into a happy marriage, but she refused to believe either that her husband was dead or that he may be unworthy. She was sure of herself and her faith in her absentee

FACING PAGE:
Madan Manjari.
The faithful and devout wife of Baba Alauddin Khan.

Madan Manjari playing the harmonium.

Boro Ma took keen interest in music and played the harmonium beautifully.

husband never wavered. When utterly surprised by her staunch loyalty to Alauddin, her brothers questioned her, she said that having been married once, there was no question of a second husband for her. Her loyalty and belief in the first was unshakable. When her annoyed relatives tried to be more forceful, Madan Manjari decided to give up her life. One night, she tried to hang herself by means of a rope tied to the bamboo support of the ceiling. Luckily for everyone, it gave way under her weight, creating a massive racket. Her mother, who was sleeping in the same room, woke up, and realizing what her daughter was up to, managed to save her life.

Still hopeful of changing her mind, her brothers tried convincing her, saying that since her husband was a Muslim, she was eligible to marry again as it was permitted in Islam. Madan Manjari stuck to her stand, reiterating that she had an unimaginable amount of trust in the bond of her marriage and it would reunite her with her husband. Finally, her brothers tried to impose their will forcefully. Madan Manjari then took to fasting and after eight days of her going hungry, everyone in the family gave up and surrendered to her resolve. She was brought to her in-laws' house to live there. Boro Baba's family members were very happy to have their daughter-in-law with them. 'She is as important and precious to us as Alauddin is,' they said. Especially after hearing how firm she had been in her faith, their pride and love for the girl strengthened many times over. However, Madan Manjari's family members were not pleased and went away fuming that their mutual relationship was severed forever. Disturbed by this state of affairs, Boro Baba's father called his older sons and told them to search for their brother. 'If Madan Manjari gives up her life, none of us can ever face the world' warned the old man.

After much investigation and timely assistance from a few sources, they were able to trace Boro Baba at Rampur under the tutelage of Ustad Wazir Khan. They also learnt (though it is not obvious how they came by this knowledge) that it was impossible to convince Boro Baba and bring him back home by any amount of reasoning or talk. The family members discussed the situation among themselves and sent a telegram directly to Ustad Wazir Khan. Its message was that Alauddin's wife, who was with them, would have committed suicide but had been dissuaded and saved, and requested the Ustad to send Alauddin back home.

Redemption

Had he known about this plot, Baba might not have approved, but it came to him as a blessing in disguise. It was only on reading this telegram that a picture of Boro Baba flashed in Wazir Khan's mind. He was the boy who had been taken as a disciple after the Nawab himself recommended his acceptance! The Ustad wondered what had happened to him. Somehow, he had completely forgotten the youngster. Suddenly awakened to this reality, Wazir Khan felt guilty and remorseful. He immediately called his three sons, Piyar Khan, Achha Sahib and Chhote Sahib (all much older than Boro Baba) and enquired about the 'Bengali boy called Alauddin'. They replied that for years the boy had been regularly coming to the entrance of the house and waiting for him at the entrance all morning, went to the band thereafter, returned in the evening to wait again for two hours. 'Oh God, then all this while why didn't any one of you teach him, at least?' asked the Ustad. 'But you never told us to!' replied one of them. Then, acceding to his father's request, Accha Sahib called Boro Baba, giving him a hint of what had happened. Boro Baba came, crying as he prostrated himself before the guru, who held him up close to his bosom and showered him with affection.

'All right, what is past is past; let us not worry about it any more, my child. You have passed the test of starvation and desperation to survive. Now we will start all over again. I shall fill the void of all these years within a short span of time,' he promised.

When asked about his family, Boro Baba revealed the truth about himself, his five brothers, and two sisters. But when the guru asked him about his marriage, he bent his head in shame, confessing the injustice he had done to his wife. Still, there was no question of his going home immediately at any cost. Even when he was told of the occurrences at home and the family's frantic search for him, Boro Baba stood firm and said, 'I have learnt nothing so far, and I don't want to go home in this condition. I can go only after I have studied and learnt music, and become an ideal human being. Then I will visit home with your permission, otherwise I will not.'

Boro Baba's devotion to the cause of music revealed much to the Ustad. It hurt his conscience to think that he had been so callous towards someone so deserving. He almost broke down and could not help confessing, 'Sorry, my child, I have conducted myself very incorrectly with you so far. It is nothing short of a sin. I hope you will pardon me for this. But I know the day you become a great musician, all my sins will be forgiven.' Wanting to make amends for his lapses, he then asked Boro Baba, 'Well, my boy, for you to become a top artiste, you must know about other achievers. Have you heard about the great *veena* and *rabab* performers of our land? Can you name them?' Boro Baba replied that one such musician was Kasim Ali Khan, from whom his father had learnt the *sitar* for a very long time.

Upon hearing that his uncle Kasim Ali Khan had taught Baba Alauddin's father, Ustad Wazir Khan was delighted and thought it was an act of divine intervention that Boro Baba had come to him to pursue music. 'You have come to just the right place to learn music, my son; by the grace of God all your wishes will surely be fulfilled. And henceforth, you are not an outsider to this place. You are my very own son – my fourth son!' said the Ustad, 'And I shall hide nothing from you. Everything belonging to the *gharana* shall be yours, as a matter of right. That will include learning the *veena*. So whatever is mine is yours for the asking.' But Boro Baba said he was content to learn the *sarode*, the *rabab* and the *surshringar*, and would not hanker after mastering the *veena*. Wazir Khan thought for a while and said, 'Well, that's very modest of you, Alauddin; still, I want to teach you everything. My sons have become rich; they do not work

any more. So I will pass on everything to you, and give *taleem* to none but you.'

Ustad Wazir Khan kept his word and, at long last, Boro Baba's full-fledged *taleem* started. Quite often, he taught Boro Baba in private and no one else was allowed to enter the premises. Boro Baba poured his heart and soul into learning from the Ustad. Music became his life and nothing else interested him. From dusk to dawn, every moment was meant for *riyaz*. In the company of Wazir Khan's sons, he learnt the *dhrupad*, the *hori*, the *tarana*, the *chaturang* and songs, and also the *sitar*, the *sarode*, the *rabab* and the *surshringar* separately. This odyssey of rigorous learning from the ustad, continued unabated for thirty-three years.

After teaching Boro Baba for all these years, Ustad Wazir Khan finally asked for *shiksha*, *diksha* and *pariksha* – learning, teaching and examination, respectively. These were the only characteristic demands of the ustads of the Senia *gharana*, who did not believe in charging any money for their teachings when a student had completed his *taleem*.

Boro Baba accompanied by his students.

Jatin Banerjee on sitar *and Timir Baran Bhattacharya on the* sarode.

Maihar – A Turning Point

9

Music isn't just learning notes and playing them, you learn notes to play to the music of your soul.

—Katie Greenwood

When Ustad Wazir Khan finally permitted Boro Baba to perform on stage, the honour became big news. Classical musicians and organizers of various music conferences such as the Tansen Music Festival, who kept track of promising musicians, had known all along, that it was only a matter of time before Boro Babu took his rightful place before a discerning audience. Gradually, he began to be known as a musical genius whose performances were a magical experience for audiences.

Boro Baba shared a musical platform with the ustads of various *gharanas* who admired him and were awed by his dexterity on various instruments. In those days, established musicians dressed splendidly, rather like maharajas, in resplendent silk turbans and gold-threaded costumes, with gold medals displayed on their chests; and then there was Boro Baba - in his unadorned cotton *dhoti* and plain white cap - he was the essence of simplicity among showmen. Among the audience one day, was the Prime Minister of Maihar, a small state located some 120 km from Khajuraho in Madhya Pradesh, founded in 1778 by the Rajputs of the Kachchwaha clan who were granted land by the ruler of the nearby state of Orchha. Maihar became a princely state of British India in the early nineteenth century and was administered as part of the Central India Agency. The Prime Minister was both surprised and intrigued to see this ordinary-looking person on stage among

Guru and *shishya*.
Boro Baba with a disciple in Madina Bhawan.

FACING PAGE:

Boro Baba in front of Madina Bhawan.

TOP:

Playing the violin in a dramatic manner to amuse his wife.

Boro Baba sharing a special moment with his wife Madina Begum.

BOTTOM:

Madina Begum posing with a *sitar*.

She used to play the harmonium and sing folk music of Bangladesh.

such august company. Once Boro Baba began playing the *sarode*, he was even more impressed. That same evening, another recital by my great-grandfather was arranged at the Maharaja of Maihar's palace in Calcutta. Boro Baba had begun only the first notes on his *sarode*, when the Maharaja, Brijnath Singh, rushed up to the stage and touched my great-grandfather's feet. He pleaded: 'You are going to be my guru. You must come and live in Maihar – I will give you a house and a salary. You have to come – I won't let you go!' He begged him repeatedly to accept the appointment. As it happened, Boro Baba needed a job to enable him to take care of his family, so he agreed.

Before he shifted to Maihar, he finally went home to his aged parents, wife, brothers and sisters, who were overjoyed to have him back among them. Shortly after he started his householder's life, his parents and elder brother passed away. Then, with the permission of the remaining family elders, he took his wife to Maihar and started living there in 1918. This was a turning point in his life, for Maihar became his home from that year till the day he died.

The Maharaja of Maihar treated Boro Baba with great veneration and continued his tutelage under him during these years. This royal patronage made it easier for Boro Baba to dedicate the rest of his life to the spread of music. His house, Madina Bhawan, built on the land gifted by the Maharaja, was designed by Boro Baba himself. However, there is no documented account of a musical performance in the Maihar palace itself, which is a pity, because there must have been many memorable recitals by Boro Baba there.

In those days, it was the live performance on stage that brought a musician recognition, but the radio, too, had become a popular

TOP:

Father and son.

Boro Baba and young Ali Akbar Khan in front of Shiva temple, Maihar.

ABOVE:

Madina Bhawan in Maihar.

Madina Bhawan was home not only to Boro Baba's family, but also to his students who could not afford lodging elsewhere.

and powerful medium. It was through the All India Radio that Boro Baba's music was heard in the homes of people all over India, the chain booking of his programmes at various AIR centres, gave him tremendous exposure.

TOP:

A view of the Maihar Palace.

ABOVE:

Maharaja of Maihar, Brijnath Singh.

He was a great patron of Indian classical music.

The Maihar Band

In 1918, there was epidemic outbreak of red fever in the state which reportedly left many people homeless and orphaned. Boro Baba was deeply moved by what he saw, and soon after, along with the Maharaja, he conceived the idea of giving musical training to several orphan children who were victims of this tragedy. Thus, began the story of India's first orchestra, a group of young boys and girls, between eight and sixteen years of age, whom Baba taught with great dedication and passion. The Maharaja lent his full support and procured various Indian and a few Western instruments for the children. Boro Baba adopted twenty-eight of them, started teaching them from scratch and gradually trained them into a band of talented instrumentalists. In those days, such a troupe of Indian musicians was a novel concept, more so because folk and Western classical music were also blended into their repertoire. Apart from the diverse musical instruments – *sitars, tablas*, cellos and clarinets – Boro Baba even created new ones for the band's use, made from inexpensive or discarded materials like rejected gun barrels.

The band would perform in the gallery above the palace Durbar Hall, where members of the royal family and other dignitaries would assemble to hear them – and Boro Baba, the band master would always be there with them. It is said that Boro Baba would often claim that no band on earth could equal the music played by this band. He taught over 250 compositions, several in just a single *raga*, building up a rich repertory for the band. He also taught them Western compositions so that Europeans who visited the Maihar court, could be entertained. The fact that he appreciated Western music is also evident from the framed sketch of Beethoven that hangs in his room in Maihar to date.

In later years, many of the band's instrumentalists, such as Sanat Banerji, Ranjit Banerji (*chandrasarang*), Shiv Balak Tiwari (*sitar*) and Shyam Bihari (*sarode*), moved on to become soloists, teachers or broadcasters. When the band needed support after Boro Baba passed away and it was left without his leadership, Narayan Singh, a member of the Maihar royal family, took the initiative and got the band attached to the Maihar Music College (Boro Babu set this institution up in 1955). Today the band is in its fifth generation, and members continue to learn and play the compositions that Boro Baba had specially created for them. The band is associated with the Department of Culture of the Madhya Pradesh government, and still performs at important state functions.

The earliest photograph of the Maihar Band, the first Indian orchestra.

The band had young and novice musicians who were orphaned during the famine. Women, too, were included in the orchestra. Boro Baba, the band master, is seated in the centre.

The Maihar Gharana

This is a relatively new *gharana* (it was created in the nineteenth century, but Baba's contribution to it was so tremendous, that he is

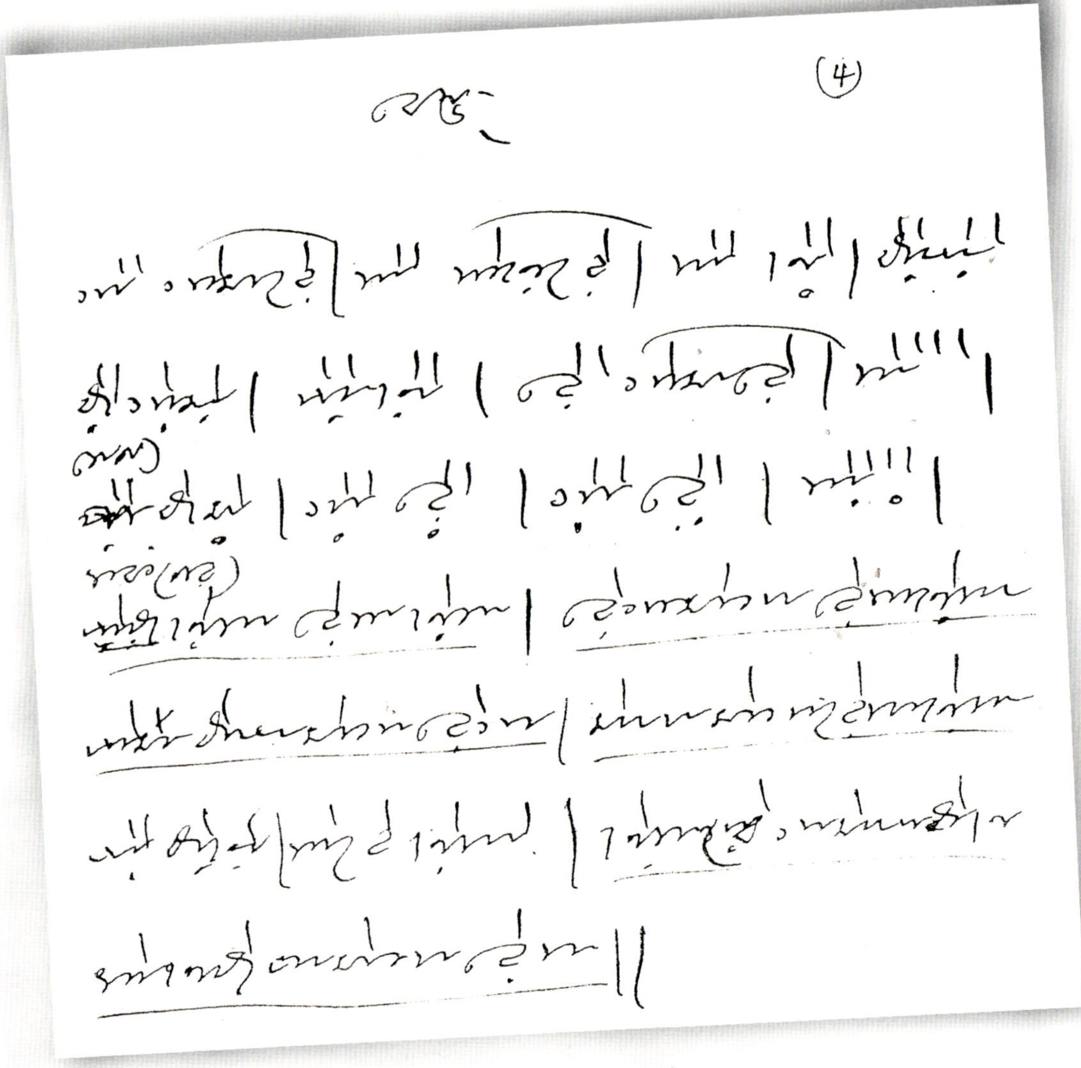

TOP:

A notation for a composition written by Baba, to be played by the Maihar Band.

LEFT:

The Maihar Band with mature players.

The naltarang *played by Jhurrelal, one of the first members of the band, is displayed in the foreground. The instrument was made from gun barrels.*

often considered to be its founder) reshaped by Boro Baba and deeply influenced by the Seni-Beenkar *gharana* of Mian Tansen, which Boro Baba's guru, Wazir Khan, belonged to. Baba incorporated the style of the Seni *gharana* to the *sarode* style that he had developed over the years. The *gharana* that subsequently evolved came to be known as Seni-Maihar or simply the Maihar *gharana*. The Maihar style is informed by the vocal *dhrupad ang*, with its elaborate *alaap* (introspective exposition), and improvisations based on *meend,* blending various musical sources. As old recordings demonstrate, previously musicians playing string instruments concentrated on only certain facets of the *raga* – there was no *alaap,* for instance, on the *sitar* and most of the phrases and *taans* were played in the rather monotonous '*diri diri*'. There were no *sapat taans* or long *meends* either. But Boro Baba made the valuable contribution of introducing the style of the *surshringar*, the *surbahar* and the *veena* to other instruments and all these techniques were amalgamated in the music of the Maihar *gharana*, in a creative innovation. It is one of those few *gharanas* in which the passing of musical traditions through the generations has not been limited to just family members, and has, in fact, been conducted more in keeping with the *guru-shishya parampara*.

Boro Baba made Maihar into a *gharana* and a seat of excellence in Indian classical music. This is, perhaps, the reason why Maihar is the only place in India, where a giant plaque at the railway station speaks of the significance of the town. The citizens of Maihar, with the help of the then railway minister, Madhavrao Scindia; himself a music aficionado and luminary of Madhya Pradesh, approached the railways to have this honour bestowed on Boro Baba.

The teacher with his disciples.

The Maihar Band learning from Boro Baba (seated on chair) in the premises of Madina Bhawan.

Globetrotter

10

Travel is more than the seeing of sights; it is a change that goes on, deep and permanent, in the ideas of living.

—Miriam Beard

In December 1934, Boro Baba performed at the All Bengal Music Conference in Calcutta, which was inaugurated by none other than Rabindranath Tagore himself. It was there that he first met Uday Shankar, who was there to perform with his well-known dancing troupe (which included his brother Ravi Shankar). Uday Shankar was the son of the renowned Sanskrit scholar and barrister, Pandit Shyam Shankar, and had earned a name for himself as an innovative choreographer and dancer. He formed his own dance troupe in 1930 and performed at the New Empire Theatre, Calcutta; an event that earned him many accolades.

He met Boro Baba for the first time at the music conference in Calcutta, and was completely taken in by his music. He knew of Baba through Timir Baran Bhattacharya, the great *sarode* player and one of the first disciples of Boro Baba. Timir Baran had joined Shankar's troupe on a successful tour of Europe and the United States in 1934 but then left after returning to India, creating a vacuum.

Entranced by Boro Baba's performance, Uday Shankar immediately requested him to join their troupe as a soloist for one year on their next European tour. At first Baba was reluctant to leave his family for so long and wanted to take his young son, Ali Akbar Khan along. As the day to set sail approached, Ali Akbar refused to go and his mother, habituated to her husband's long absences, was probably not too keen either. Hemangini Devi,

FACING PAGE:
A rare moment of idleness.
Baba smoking a cigar.

Uday Shankar's mother, entrusted her younger son Ravi Shankar in Alauddin's care, symbolically putting her son's hands in his. Alauddin became a father figure to Ravi Shankar and came to be called Baba; a name that would stay with him for the rest of his life.

Boro Baba left with the troupe in November 1935. It was his first trip overseas and he was amazed at the scientific progress of the West, even as the hospitality of people overwhelmed him. His experiences and feelings are reflected in the letters he wrote to his younger brothers, Ayet Ali Khan and Nayeb Ali Khan, during this period. These simple epistles may not be the work of a literary genius, but they are a powerful evocation of Boro Baba's thoughts. They also tell us a great deal about the person he was; simple, full of zest for life and an eagerness to constantly learn new lessons.

On one occasion, he wrote to Ayet Ali Khan from England, saying:

'I am sending a photograph of mine, dressed in an English suit. I feel ashamed in front of the gentlemen here if I am not dressed like that. I have to wear this dress if I have to move about and dine with them. It is terrible – I don't know English, so I remain seated like a mute. I take the help of the interpreters. Everyone praises the instrument made by you. They were also impressed with the *chandrasarang* and its tenor. Renowned musicologists came to see it and were pleased with its music. They consider it to be superior even to the *sarode*, considering its *gat* and *meend*. I once told them that the piano was also a good instrument, but they didn't agree. They insisted that Indian musical instruments were better and rendered sweeter music.'

Another time, he wrote from Paris:

'I have arrived in Paris after visiting Arabia, Greece, Switzerland, Budapest, Vienna, Prague and Germany. After

Boro Baba

Boro Baba at his adda; a room in Madina Bhawan.

FACING PAGE TOP:

In Europe, like the Europeans!

Baba during his European tour with Uday Shankar's dance troupe in 1935–36.

FACING PAGE BOTTOM:

Boro Baba's youngest brother, Ayet Ali Khan.

He assisted Baba in constructing new instruments. Boro Baba shared a deep bond with Ayet Ali Khan and wrote letters to him from abroad.

this, I shall visit Belgium, and move to London for three months. Then, I shall go to America. I am entering a new phase of life after visiting these countries. It is hard to believe that all these things are created by human beings. Everything seems so strange – houses, cities, roads, gardens, museums, parks, zoos and so on. The trains here run on three levels – the underground, ground level and overhead. Whatever you see above and on ground, you would find underground as well. Quite unbelievable!'

'...Athens, Vienna, Budapest, Prague and other cities hold the cradle of music. Reputed professors talked to me after listening to my *sarode*. They all loved the music and newspapers gave me a wide coverage. Many people took my photograph.'

Boro Baba also went to the countryside in Europe and keenly observed the way of life there. Indeed, he was very impressed with their advanced farming and dairy methods, hygiene, educational standards, awareness and even their devoutness, all of which he passionately describes in his letters. Yet, he missed the familiarity of his country:

'I have become weak for want of food. They eat mostly ham here. I only eat boiled potatoes, boiled peas, butter, bread and fruits. I feel like vomiting at the smell of half-baked food. Uday Shankar Babu is worried at this. He is trying to send me home. I am not stationed at one place. I travel around many countries. It is not possible to cook my own food. People here cannot think of living without drinking wine and eating meat. They drink wine like water.'

However busy he was while on tour, Boro Baba always had the youngsters of the family in mind and monitored their progress constantly. In a letter from Palestine, he asks about his son, Ali Akbar:

'Advise Ali Akbar to continue his practise and studies. He should not waste time. There should be no lapses in his education. Educate him, even if you have to beg for his fees. I shall meet you on my return home. I seek God's blessings.'

For the benefit of those at home, he described in detail all the new and fascinating things he saw and experienced:

A young Boro Baba, dressed as a nawab.

FACING PAGE:

In a pensive mood.

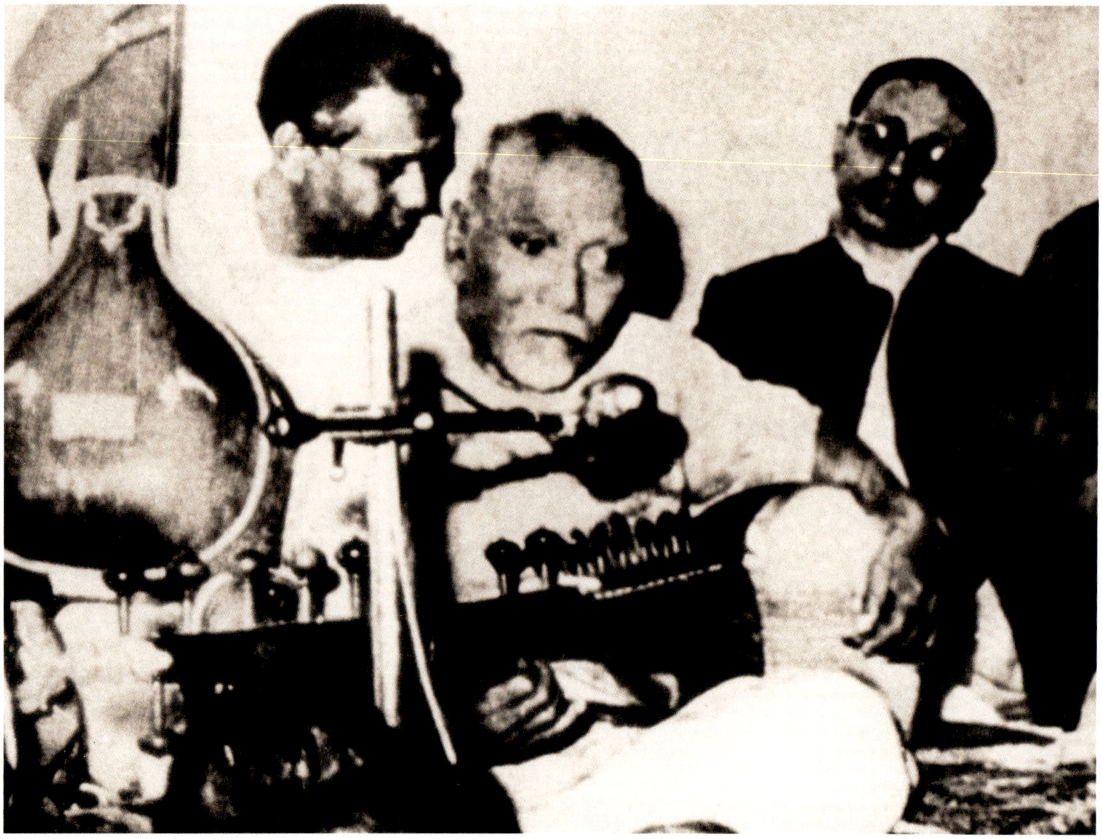

Boro Baba at a live concert in Calcutta.

'Now I have come to an Arab country from Africa. I saw Jesus Christ's birthplace and also where he was crucified... What our *maulvis* used to say, about there being no musical activity in Arabia, is not correct. All people here, irrespective of religion, sing and play music; I have seen their musical instruments. Muslims play something like our *dotara*, while the people of other religions play on western instruments.'

'I may not be bringing home money, but I am satisfied at seeing things around. I will return after a year, whatever happens. People have to spend so much money to see things abroad, while I am seeing them free of cost!'

As he performed and keenly watched others' concerts and exchanged ideas, Boro Baba learnt and planned improvisations in the construction of instruments. Writing to Ayet Ali Khan, he expressed his ideas for the latter to improve upon and execute:

'I am thinking of using our country instrument as a base in place of the violin. I am planning to use the lower part of the *sarangi* or *esraj* and the upper part of the *chandrasarang*. The lower gourd should be of thin plank for louder sound. Then, the *esraj* in place of the violin – about a metre long. Think of making such an instrument. I will collaborate with you when I come back. There will also be a *sitar*, small *sitars*. If you can make these, God will have fulfilled my wishes. You are intelligent. You will gain by it. I am sending some sketches I have made. Try the one you like best. You must use separate planks like those for violins. It should be a unique instrument. I shall try to come back as soon as possible. I have seen enough, to my fullest satisfaction. I have travelled a lot.'

In 1937, Uday Shankar was given a hero's welcome when he visited Calcutta after his tour in Europe and the United States and Rabindranath Tagore came to meet him personally. In 1939, with the encouragement of Tagore, Uday Shankar established an institute called the Shankar India Cultural Centre at Almora, in the Himalayan foothills. He invited many renowned gurus to work in the Centre with him, such as Kandappa Pillai for Bharat Natyam and Amobi Singh for Manipuri dance, and Boro Baba was requested to teach music there too. Soon the Centre became the meeting place of various schools of Indian dance and music and Boro Babu would often travel to Almora to carry out his responsibilities.

Despite all the adulation he received and his many responsibilities as a teacher, Boro Baba remained a simple man whose only aim in life was the pursuit of music.

Musical Ambassador

11

The universe is full of magical things, patiently waiting for our wits to grow sharper.

—Eden Phillpotts

Boro Baba travelled to numerous countries and saw many things that bewildered and fascinated him; but what livened him up the most in the course of his travels, was music. He was surprised to note the high esteem accorded to music in foreign societies, as reflected by the huge and magnificent auditoriums and the way a great artist was applauded and honoured. He enjoyed Western music, played by bands consisting of hundreds of men and women.

Whenever he played, the response that he received from the commoners as well as connoisseurs was beyond his expectations. He was thrilled to perform before spell-bound audiences, sometimes over 4000-strong, who sat breathlessly throughout the presentation and later kept applauding for over ten minutes, showering bouquets on the stage to show their appreciation.

Once, a group of young American and European professional dancers approached Boro Baba and requested him to explain the subtleties of Indian classical music to them. Glancing at their fashionable attire, Boro Baba decided that their intentions were far from serious and therefore, casually strummed a part of *Raga Multani*, a deeply moving composition, on his *sarode*. After playing for a bit, he glanced up and was amazed to see his audience visibly moved; some of them actually had tears rolling down their cheeks. Ashamed of his biased judgment, he instantly started performing with intense concentration. He played *Raga Bhimpalasree* and *Raga Pilu* for over three hours, and his flawless rendition led the

FACING PAGE:

Boro Baba at Madina Bhawan.

Boro Baba gave to his students all he had. In return, he was showered with respect and love.

Engrossed in an atmosphere full of melody.

Auditoriums were always packed when Boro Baba performed.

listeners to exclaim, 'You have given us life. We will never forget it.'

On yet another occasion in Budapest, Boro Baba lectured some European intellectuals on the finer nuances of Indian classical music. Ravi Shankar acted as the interpreter. On being asked whether he composed music, Boro Baba replied, 'No one composes our music. European music has to be composed. But ours can be improvised. Whatever mood comes in our mind, we try to express that.' When the foreigners expressed their inability to understand this concept, Boro Baba picked up his *sarode* and started playing *Raga Bhairavi*. When he had finished, he looked around and asked, 'What did you understand?' The responses to his query were varied. One of them felt as if the entire group was offering prayers at some church, while another was reminded of a futile wait for someone in the early hours of the morning. A third person demanded to know why Boro Baba's music sketched such sad tones. In explanation, Boro Baba said, 'We too have twelve *swaras* in an octave, seven *shuddha* like the major

scale, four *komal* and the fifth note *madhyam* is *tivra*, all the five are what you call semi-tones. But within the octave, there are twenty-two *shrutis*, which are used in different *ragas*, sometimes directly and sometimes as an embellishment or *andolan*. There are differences between the paces of each shruti. After *Sa* we have *Re*. There are four *shrutis* in between. We can differentiate these four intricate *shrutis* and express the appropriate mood.'

But his avid audience requested him to play again. Boro Baba then played every *shruti* on his *sarode*, a fact which surprised the Europeans who claimed that a high degree of sensitivity must be required to catch the minute differences between the *shrutis* with such accuracy.

Boro Baba replied, 'Certainly! That is why our *ragas* and *raginis* are so sweet and musical. There is no interference of unsound tunes. Your music has twelve *swaras* and two *talas* namely 4/8 and 6/8. Apart from these twenty-two micro-tones, we have twenty-one *murchhanas* and thousands of *ragas*, which are melodic forms and are much more developed than 'scales' or 'modes'. We have three hundred and sixty *talas*.'

All of them asked, 'How do you remember all these *talas*?'

Boro Baba in a concert.

Boro Baba with grandson Aashish Khan on the sarode.

Boro Baba then proceeded to demonstrate the different *talas* on his *tabla*, till they were satisfied. While bidding them farewell, Ustad Alauddin Khan said, 'I am honoured that you came to a simple and humble musician like me to know about our music. My knowledge of classical music, however, is very little. Please do not judge our music by listening to mine. Our ancestors could bring rain with their music, light fires, make flowers blossom. I cannot make rain with my music, cannot light a fire, nor can I make flowers blossom. If, however, you are pleased, it is due to the quality of our music, not because of my playing. You would have realized its supreme pleasure had you listened to a great musician. But I could not make it so. Please do pardon me.'

Amazed by this great man's humility, the Europeans exclaimed, 'You are a wonder of the East in our eyes!'

It was his towering ambition and strong determination which took Ustad Alauddin Khan to the peak of excellence in music. As such, he commanded great respect from people all around the world. Once, Boro Baba was performing at an international musical conference in Dhaka in 1954–55 on the invitation of the then Pakistan government. A group of dancers from Burma entered Boro Baba's room in a single, orderly file, sought his blessings and left in the

Baba with his disciples.

Boro Baba's disciples considered him their guru, mentor and father.

same dignified fashion just before they were scheduled to go onstage.

At home in India, too, Boro Baba had an avid following; he was revered and feted by ordinary citizens who got the chance to hear him perform. On a winter evening in Calcutta in the late 1950s, the season of music festivals, such as the All India Music Conference, Tansen Music Conference and Alauddin Music Conference. Boro Baba's *sarode* recital was an indispensable part of all these dusk-to-dawn programmes lasting four to five days. And it was usually scheduled for the later part, around three o'clock. There was always a heavy rush at the festivals and those who were unable to procure tickets would throng the pavements for the entire night, enjoying the music through the loudspeakers, which were installed outside for them, a reflection of how popular classical music was at the time. Boro Baba would enter the hall at around midnight and would be caught in a melee of adoring fans. One particular night, when he got out of his car, he was almost mobbed by a crowd of his fans and disciples, all eager to show their regard for the genius. As the group swelled, Boro Baba had to literally push himself through to the dais. It was a mammoth effort but he did not say anything. It was an unbridled show of the love people had for their musical idol.

Baba's love for music is present in his timeless compositions.

Boro Baba with his disciples.

The Teacher and His Students

12

A teacher affects eternity. He can never tell where his influence stops.

—Henry Brookes Adams

The illustrious disciples of Boro Baba include his talented daughter Annapurna Devi; his son, Ustad Ali Akbar Khan; the prodigious Pandit Ravi Shankar, who was also his son-in-law; his grandson Aashish Khan; nephew Ustad Bahadur Khan; Pandit Nikhil Banerjee; Smt. Sharan Rani; Pandit Pannalal Ghosh and Timir Baran Bhattacharya – to mention a few. These disciples in turn created the next generation of classical artists like Hari Prasad Chaurasia, Brijbhushan Kabra, Satyadev Pawar and Vinay Bharat Ram.

His son, Ali Akbar Khan, who is my Dadu (paternal grandfather in Bengali), says, 'We believe that music leads the way to God. The spiritual quality of music affects one's whole life. For us as a family, music is like food. When you need it, you don't have to explain why, because it is basic to life.' Dadu's own quest for perfection through music commenced at the age of three, in his native town of Bangladesh, when his father began teaching him the rudiments of singing. Within a few years, Boro Baba had determined that the boy should concentrate on vocal performance and on playing the *sarode*.

'When I was very young, my father would sit with me for fifteen hours a day, correcting me every second,' recalls Dadu. He very aptly compares his tutelage with that of the great golfer Tiger Woods, 'One thinks of the child Tiger Woods, swinging a golf club

FACING PAGE:

Boro Baba teaching his son and disciple, Ali Akbar Khan, at Madina Bhawan.

Boro Baba was not partial to any of his students – he never gave his son preferential treatment over other students and gave the same rigorous training to all.

BELOW LEFT:

Boro Baba's second daughter, Jahanara.

She died a tragic death in Maihar, a few years after her marriage into an orthodox family from Dhaka who opposed her attempts to pursue music.

BELOW RIGHT:

Deeply devoted to music.

Boro Baba and Annapurna in Maihar.

hour after hour under his father's critical eye until the club became an extension of the mind and body of the child.' So it was with Dadu, whose waking hours were devoted to learning *ragas* – not just imbibing tunes but mastering what a Westerner might call interpretation.

'Each note is like the centre of an ocean,' Dadu says, 'and it is not easy to get your footing. But if the pitch is perfect and the note is approached correctly, both the player and the listener experience a response from the soul and the mind.'

'My father lived for 110 years. He was like a larger-than-life saint who lived his whole life for music. We say, if someone can play or sing the right kind of music, the door to God is always open.'

Annapurna Devi, Jahanara, Ali Akbar and Ravi Shankar

Annapurna Devi was possibly Boro Baba's biggest contribution to Indian classical music. Named after the Hindu goddess of prosperity and abundance by Brijnath Singh, the Maharaja of Maihar, Annapurna grew up in the shadow of her older sister's

tragic demise. Boro Baba's elder daughter, Jahanara, had grown up in an atmosphere charged with classical music but was married into a family that disapproved of her interests totally. Her in-laws abused and threatened her to the point where, barely ten months after her marriage, an emaciated and emotionally exhausted Jahanara gave up her life in Madina Begum's arms. Unable to put this horrific incident behind him, Boro Baba swore that he would never teach music to another daughter. However, he exerted himself tirelessly to coach his young son, Ali Akbar, in the rich classical traditions of the Maihar *gharana*. On one occasion, irritated with Ali Akbar's lack of concentration, Boro Baba decided to go to the market to cool his wrath. However, halfway to his destination, he turned back as he had forgotten his wallet. The moment he stepped into the house, he heard little Annapurna's clear, bell-like tones instructing Ali Akbar to play the *taan* correctly. This was the beginning of Annapurna's training, which led to her emergence as one of the foremost instrumentalists in the field of Indian classical music.

Another prodigious talent that flourished under Boro Baba's able guidance was Ravi Shankar. Ravi Shankar first met Boro Baba when the latter was touring the West with Uday Shankar's dance troupe in 1935. Boro Baba taught Ravi traditional songs, albeit in a sketchy

ABOVE:

Boro Baba with his disciples who carried forward his lineage across seven seas.

Ali Akbar Khan (extreme left), Ravi Shankar (extreme right) and Baba (second from right).

LEFT:

Annapurna Devi and Ravi Shankar.

Annapurna Devi with husband, Ravi Shankar, playing the surbahar.

Boro Baba with his disciples and fans.

Sitting with Baba, from left to right, are Ravi Shankar, Hirendra Kumar Ganguli and Ali Akbar Khan.

fashion, on board ships during the summers of 1935 and 1936. This sporadic training made Ravi Shankar yearn for more and, after Boro Baba had left the troupe to teach Ali Akbar, he arrived at Maihar to be taken on as a disciple. He also underwent rigorous training and Baba lost his temper once when his disciple could not grasp a complicated passage, saying, 'You are like a weak little girl!' Ravi Shankar packed his bags to leave in a huff, but Boro Baba said, 'If you go, it'll hurt me very much. You are like a son to me.' Ravi Shankar stayed on and Boro Baba never scolded him again. Later, Uday Shankar broached the topic of Annapurna's marriage to his brother, and Boro Baba acquiesced, despite initial misgivings.

Modes of Training

A superhuman power lies dormant in every human being, but he has to be inspired and aroused to enjoy this exalted feeling of oneness with God by developing his creative faculties, whether spiritual, musical or poetic. This is why Boro Baba advised his disciples to tenaciously pursue purity of the body and mind in addition to single-minded *sadhana*. He pleaded for *swara-sadhana* and declared that even with his best efforts, he experienced the eternal bliss of communicating with God through music, only on rare occasions in his life.

In the initial stages of studentship, Boro Baba trained all his students in vocal and instrumental music simultaneously. Along with *swara-sadhana*, the practise of instrumental music was continued for at least three years. He mainly stressed upon *Raga Bhairavi* in the morning, *Yaman* in the evening and *Kafi* between the two. The various *thats* were taught by continuous training for years, together with *bols*. Along with lessons on *meend*, the knowledge of *krintan*, *gamak*, etc., was also imparted for fairly long durations.

At first, he started with the *sargam*, which was followed by the proper formation of *gats*. When these were memorized, vocal music was taken up, followed by instrumental music. It was imperative for students to learn the *tarana* by heart. This system called for regular practise for years on end, with unwavering devotion and dedication.

After the completion of these preliminaries, Boro Baba himself would sing and play on instruments; this was to be reproduced by his disciples, which helped him assess the depth of their learning. He rectified the minor mistakes but would not forgive major faults. Thus his students acquired complete mastery over *shruti*, *raga*, *chalan* and *vadi-samvadi*. The training of *laya* was offered through *gatkari*. The students also had to undergo considerable training in the tabla and the *pakhawaj* and display it before Baba. Thereafter, the training of *gat*

BELOW:

Boro Baba with disciple and son-in-law, Ravi Shankar.

BOTTOM:

Ravi Shankar embracing *gurubhai* and brother-in-law, Ali Akbar Khan.

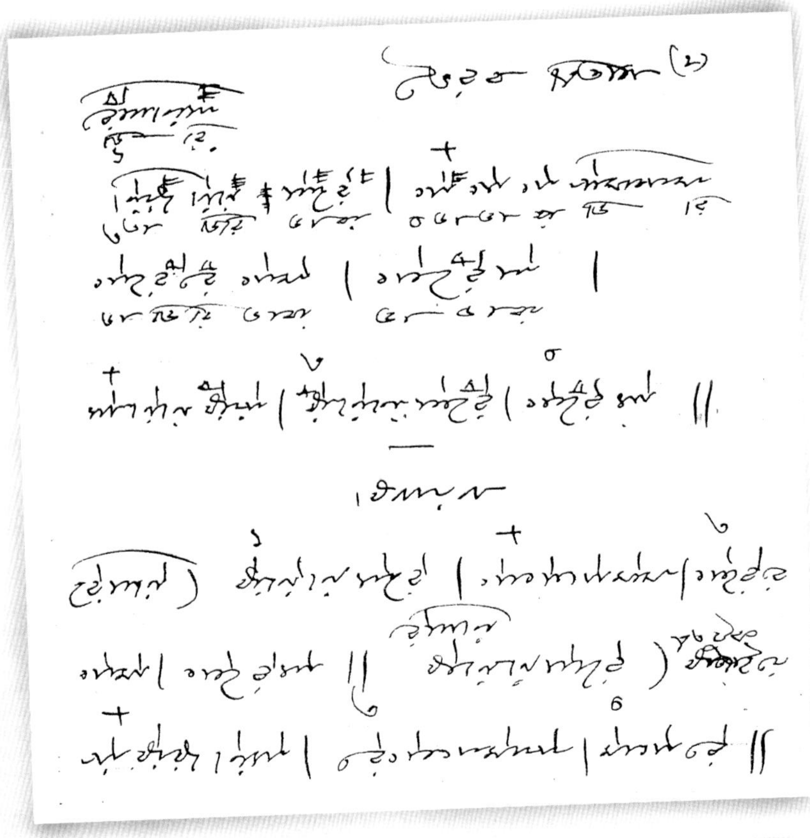

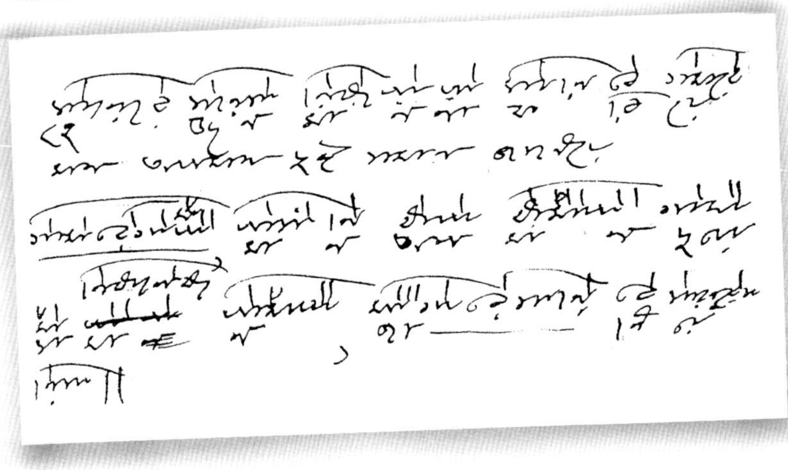

TOP:

Boro Baba in a classroom full of students.

Boro Baba on the tabla *and Ali Akbar on the* sarode *during a class in Ali Akbar's music college in Maihar.*

BOTTOM:

Boro Baba with his fans.

Boro Baba displaying the chandrasarang *to some music lovers after a concert.*

FACING PAGE:

Notation for *Raga Bhairavi* as composed by Baba.

The most popular morning raga *in north Indian classical music.*

RIGHT:

With Nikhil Banerjee, who played the *sitar*.

Banerjee met Boro Baba in 1947. He went to Boro Baba's concerts and followed him around, and in the end, even went so far as to threaten to kill himself if he was not accepted as a disciple. Boro Baba did not want to take on more students, but changed his mind after listening to one of Banerjee's radio broadcasts.

BELOW:

Sharan Rani Backliwal, Boro Baba's disciple.

Sharan Rani recalls how Boro Baba had an open house and never took any fee for teaching.

followed in different *talas*. Separate *gats* were taught along with *tan*, *tora* and *laykari*. At times, Baba played on the tabla and his students had to practise with him for hours. Finally, Baba took his students on to playing the *alaap*, to which he attached the greatest importance. This was when the students were introduced to the nine moods, or *nava-rasas*, the traditional classification of thematic content in arts in India. The *alaap* was the embodiment of *karuna* as the crescendo raised into *jod* and *jhala*; the others, *shringara*, *veera* and *rasa*, also were manifest in music. This was Baba's interpretation. Some of his popular *ragas* were *Yaman*, *Hemanta*, *Hem-Behag*, *Tilak Kamod*, *Shree*, *Vilawal*, *Durbari*, *Shudh Basant*, *Puria Dhanesri*, *Shudh Bhairo* and *Shudh Kalyan*.

Boro Baba laid great emphasis on the time at which the *ragas* were played and practised; this is still followed in our family.

TOP:

Boro Baba teaching the Maharaja of Maihar.

The patronage of the Maharaja helped Boro Baba realize his dream.

BOTTOM:

Boro Baba with his students.

Timir Baran Bhattacharya (left), Boro Baba's first sarode *student and Radhika Mohan Moitra (right), with Boro Baba.*

Innovator of Music and Instruments

13

Deeds, not stones, are the true monuments of the great.

—John L. Motley

While India had always been a treasure house of musical traditions over the centuries, the precious gemstones of Hindustani music were the exclusive property of a few *gharanas*, and not easily accessible to 'outsiders'. Another imbalance was that vocal music had completely overshadowed instrumental music. The latter, in spite of its hoary history and the astounding variety it provided, had been relegated to an inferior position. It was Alauddin Khan who set right both these discrepancies. He was greatly responsible for popularizing instrumental music. He had learnt music with tremendous effort and under unbelievable hardships; he discovered its basic technical structure and also developed scientific methods for its teaching.

Though Boro Baba preferred to play the *rabab*, the violin and the *surshringar*, his principal performing instrument was the *sarode*. He made several improvisations on it that helped execute ragas in refined and perfect ways. His innovations also allowed one to play ragas on the *surshringar*, amalgamating characteristics of both the *rabab* and the veena in terms of pitch and sound. In the early twentieth century, the *surshringar* consisted of sixteen strings (three lower, three upper, one *chikari*

Instruments preserved at Baba's living room in Maihar.

FACING PAGE:

Looking back at life.

Baba in his room surrounded by instruments created by him and Ayet Ali Khan.

and nine *taraf*). Baba added ten more strings, bringing the total to twenty-six (four lower, five upper, two *chikari*, and fifteen *taraf*). He also enlarged the size and changed the shape of the *tumba*. Besides the *sarode*, Boro Baba could play a variety of instruments. He was comfortable with the violin, the clarinet, the trumpet, the cornet, the flute, the drums, the harmonium, the piano, the *esraj*, the *dilruba*, the *pakhawaj*, the tabla, drums and the *dhol*. He improvised with the style of playing on many of these. More importantly, he devised and introduced several new instruments, creating the *chandrasarang* and developing the *sitar* banjo, a combination of the two instruments played by a string peak. Then he made the *nal tarang* from gun barrels which is played with a piece of iron. He replaced the wooden plate of the *sarindra* with a metal one and effected other improvements.

Boro Baba gave the *sarode* a new form because he realized that in its traditional form it was not suitable for the *dhrupad* style. In collaboration with his brother, Ustad Ayet Ali Khan, he made several modifications. Among other things, he added the *jawari* strings to catch the appropriate notes of the *raga*, and two *chikaris* to be tuned to the higher register of the tonic *sa*. He also changed the bridge on the parchment which holds three layers of strings, enlarged the parchment and standardized the thickness of the goat-skin attached to the parchment, as well as that of the steel plate on the finger board.

ABOVE:

The skeleton of a sarode, *as modified by Baba and followed by the Maihar Senia* gharana.

RIGHT:

Chandrasarang.

FACING PAGE:

Boro Baba playing various instruments.

Musician Par Excellence

Alauddin Khan is remembered as a master player of the *sarode* but not enough is known of his contributions in many related fields.

His exceptional skill enriched the musical world and his talent for creating ragas was unsurpassed. Not many people have an idea of the creations and innovations that he made in ragas and instruments. *Ragas* created by him are played by musicians everywhere, but not recognized as such. Here is a long list of these: *Bhagabati, Bhuvaneswari, Chandika, Dhabalsri, Durgeswari, Gandhi-Bilawal, Haimanti, Hemant, Hemant-Bhairav, Hem-Bihag, Kaushi, Kedar-Manjh, Madan Manjari* (named after his dear wife), *Madavgiri, Manj-Khammaj, Kedar-Manj, Megh-Bahar, Muhammad, Nagarjun, Prabhakali, Prabhatkeli Rabindra, Rajasri, Sobhavati, Sugandh, Saraswati,* and *Umabati.* While many modern musicians knowingly pass off many of these as *prachalita* ragas, a large number are not even aware of who created them and when.

Boro Baba also composed music for innumerable songs. His songs, with notations, used to be regularly published in magazines. He was also an able lyricist and wrote under the name 'Alam' which was how he was fondly addressed by his family.

TOP LEFT:

Baba receiving an award.

TOP RIGHT:

Boro Baba receiving the Padma Vibhushan from President V. V. Giri in 1971.

BOTTOM:

Baba receiving the Desikottam award in a special convocation held in Shanti Niketan in 1961.

FACING PAGE TOP (LEFT):

Boro Baba's body being taken out of Madina Bhawan for the funeral.

FACING PAGE TOP (RIGHT):

Boro Baba's and Boro Ma's mausoleum in Maihar.

FACING PAGE BOTTOM:

Ali Akbar Khan performing in his father's memory.

Accompanied by Kishan Maharaj on tabla, *Nikhil Banerjee on* sitar *and Dhyanesh Khan on the* sarode.

Alauddin Khan – Remembered by Family

14

Indian music is like a river or stream that has come down to us through time, bringing nurture to man's soul. From the past masters, this music flowed to my father and through him to me. I want to keep this stream flowing. I don't want it to die. It must spread all over the world.

—Ali Akbar Khan

Baba Alauddin Khan's eldest grandson and Ali Akbar Khan's first son, Aashish Khan, who is an eminent *sarode* maestro himself, reminisces about his 'Guru and Dadu (grandfather)', who meant everything to him. He says that he owes everything that he is today, to the strict discipline, training and 'so many more things which cannot be aptly expressed in words' that he received from Boro Baba. He recalls how Boro Baba was prone to a quick temper but this anger was only during the *taleem* period. The reason was more than just noble – he expected his disciples to be as dedicated and unparalleled as him. Needless to say, he had set standards for them, often as high as those he set for himself, which were but naturally beyond the capabilities of most. Aashish Khan remembers how Baba Alauddin, his 'Dadu' (grandfather) would sometimes become impatient and irritable:

'I have been very forgetful since childhood. It was common for me to forget compositions taught to me some days

FACING PAGE:

Family members remember Boro Baba for his deep love and great sense of humour.

With the younger lot.

Boro Baba with his eldest grandson, Aashish Khan, holding a miniature sarode *in his hand.*

FACING PAGE:

Past, Present and Future.

Boro Baba with his son, Ali Akbar Khan and grandson, Aashish Khan.

earlier. So whenever Dadu asked me to play a composition he had taught me, and I didn't play it correctly, he got furious. There were times when I have been beaten by him as well. Dadu's teachings are nothing short of divine. He instilled enough confidence in me as a young boy to accompany him in public concerts attended by thousands of people. My most memorable concert remains the Tansen Music Conference in Calcutta, 1952, when my grandfather, father and I filled the air with the music of three generations.'

Aashish Khan's brother Pranesh Khan, percussionist and Boro Baba's third grandson, came to live in Maihar at a very young age. Everyday, after lunch, he and his siblings would spend the afternoon in Baba's bedroom. He remembers the time when his sister would massage Baba's feet while he read a book and the

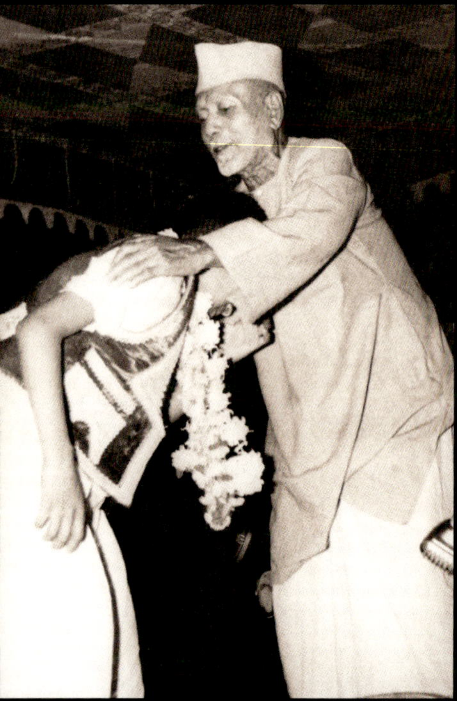

brothers would be busy playing. Their presence never bothered him and soon, Baba would fall asleep while the children quietly left the room. A renowned *tabla* player today, Pranesh Khan recalls the time when he was initiated into music by Baba Alauddin himself.

'I do not recall my age– maybe I was four or five years old. Anyway, I was running around in the courtyard when Dadu suddenly called out my name. I went to him. He was sitting with a dholak. He asked me to sit across him, played something simple on it and asked me to copy the sound. I copied it exactly and I still remember his smile – a very delighted grandfather indeed. He was a left-handed *sarode* player but a right-handed drummer. As we were trading phrases, he did not turn the drum around for me and I guess that is how I became a left-handed drummer. Soon I was playing the *tabla* and practising with my sister and my brother. Then one day he called me to his room and began teaching me the *surshringar*, the *rabab* and the *pakhawaj*. I used to play the *rabab* and the *surshringar* in his bedroom and the *pakhawaj* in his living room. Lessons were not long, maybe half-an-hour on each instrument,

and I did not mind. Whatever he asked me to play, I played diligently. I think I was just learning to strum the strings with the plectrum. This continued for a while. He never shouted at me. He would first show me what to play and then walk away from the room.

One day, a mischievous thought came to my mind – to test him if he was really listening to my playing. I must have got bored repeating the same phrase for a long time. I think no one has ever dared to do this, but knowingly, I played a phrase incorrectly on the *pakhawaj*. I knew he was on the other side of the courtyard and no sooner had I played the phrase wrong than I heard a loud yell! I was satisfied and began playing correctly. I think he knew

The legend lives on through his disciples.

Boro Baba with Aashish Khan in a concert.

FACING PAGE TOP:

The happy grandfather.

Boro Baba felicitating Aashish Khan after a concert.

FACING PAGE BOTTOM:

Boro Baba at a live concert accompanied by his disciples.

Ali Akbar Khan, Nikhil Banerjee, and Aashish Khan with Boro Baba.

exactly what I was trying, because he never came to the room to scold me.'

Khan remembers another time when he sat in the doorway and watched Baba Alauddin instructing 'Indranil-da' (Indranil Bhattacharya) in his bedroom. When he caught Indranil playing a *bol* incorrectly, Baba struck him mildly on his head with his hookah pipe saying "Da-diri diri diri da-r da-r da." Thus it went on but then Indranil pulled a string in a higher octave, which sounded like someone had just passed air. 'Dadu looked at me and said, "*Paida disay, paida disay*! (He farted!)" and began laughing. Poor Indranil-da had a hard time controlling his laughter but he hid his face behind the *sitar* and smiled at me.'

Another incident which Pranesh Khan remembered vividly involves his 'Mejda' (Bengali term for second oldest brother), Dhyanesh Khan, who played football and was an excellent goalkeeper who represented Maihar. One day, during the last moments of the final tournament match between Maihar and Rewa, Baba Alauddin suddenly appeared behind the goalkeeper, who was his grandson, Dhyanesh Khan. Pranesh Khan recalls how 'the spectators were all excited; suspense and anxiety peppered the air. Obviously, the goalkeeper had to be extremely alert. At that moment, Dadu reached there and started shouting along with the energetic crowd, but he was telling Mejda that he might break his hand playing football and would not be able to play the *sarode*! Dadu wrecked Mejda's concentration and he was in a total dilemma.' The result – Maihar lost.

In 1968, before leaving for the USA, when Pranesh Khan went to see his grandfather to receive his blessings, he knew it was the last time he would ever see him. When he was alone in Baba's room, looking at the picture of Ramakrishna Paramahamsa on the dressing table, Baba asked him to put his palm forward so he could see it. 'I did and he said, "*Tui sat samudra tero nadi paar hobi.*" (You will travel abroad)'

Pranesh Khan remembers his Dadu as a man with an abundance of understanding, expression and humour. 'His only fault, if you

Boro Baba and Aashish Khan.

Jethu considers himself blessed for being born at a time when Boro Baba could manage to give him enough attention. Boro Baba's age and health did not allow him to take an interest in his other grandchildren as he managed for Jethu.

consider it one, was that he wanted to give his students whatever he had learned in music through extreme physical, mental and emotional toil,' he says. As a teacher, Baba Alauddin did not want his students to experience the humiliation that he had faced in his time. His motto in life – "Take as much music as you want from me."

According to Pranesh Khan, the greatest thing about his grandfather, Baba Alauddin was that he taught every student in a different style; so that when they bloomed in the garden of music, each would be unique and stand apart from the rest. He taught

A concert to remember.

Baba accompanied by Kanthe Maharaj and Kishan Maharaj on the tabla, *Ravi Shankar on the* sitar *and Ali Akbar Khan on the* sarode.

Siblings in soulful symphony.

Aashish Khan flanked by Dhyanesh Khan and Pranesh Khan after a performance. His grandsons ensured that they proved their mettle as the descendants of Ustad Alauddin Khan.

them in a style that suited their personality. 'Think and compare the style of music between Aashish Khan and Ali Akbar Khan, or Ali Akbar Khan and Pandit Ravi Shankar, or Pandit Ravi Shankar and Nikhil Banerjee. One has to be a genius to achieve this particular level of sensitivity in instructing individual students and, indeed, he was one.' observes Khan.

Speaking of styles of playing, Pranesh Khan recalls an incident which occurred at the Tansen Music Festival in Calcutta, where *tabla* maestro Pandit Kishan Maharaj was performing with Baba Alauddin: 'Their (Pandit Kishan Maharaj and Ustad Alauddin Khan's) recordings together, sounded like 'musical wars' because

their styles were so different. Anyway, Dadu (Bengali for paternal grandfather) was keeping the *gat* and Kishan Maharaj began playing in his usual style in *dadra aang*. Dadu suddenly put down his *sarode* and with a mischievous smile, began making dancing gestures with his hands. The auditorium burst into laughter. Swaying his index finger from side to side, Dadu said, "*Yeh nahi chalega! Yeh nahi chalega*! (This won't do)" Poor Kishan Maharaj ji! The *tabla* is no instrument to hide behind and it was difficult for him to hide his embarrassment. But Panditji was very sporting. He did not take it seriously and the concert ended on a happy note.

As the eldest granddaughter in my generation, it was almost natural that I was adored and loved by my grandparents, besides all others in the family. It used to be a veritable party for me during the winter vacation when my Dadu (Ali Akbar Khan) came to see us in India.

One story he loved to tell us was about how he cheated on his *sarode* practise. Boro Baba's students were expected do rigorous practise for almost eighteen hours a day. There was a time in the first half of the day, when he (Ali Akbar Khan) sat down for practise. Around this time, Boro Baba would go to the market, asking them to continue their *riyaz*. Dadu was the defaulter as he would cheat and sneak out to have a puff of tobacco, while his sister Annapurna sincerely carried on her riyaz. As soon as he saw his father approaching, Ali Akbar would start playing the *sarode* again. Still he got caught most of the time as he would be playing a stage in the *riyaz*, which would not occur after the lapse of so much time. Thus, Boro Baba never failed to keep a tab on his students' progress. According to Dadu, his most sincere student was Annapurna. Normally, when the three (Ali Akbar, Annapurna and Ravi Shankar) sat down to learn from Baba, it was mostly Annapurna who played the tune most correctly and perfectly.

I spent most of my childhood with my grandmother (Zubeda Khan) and cherished all the stories she narrated periodically. She was married at the young age of nine and still has clear memories

TOP:

My grandfather, Ali Akbar Khan, and myself.

BOTTOM:

My grandmother, Zubeda Khan, and myself.

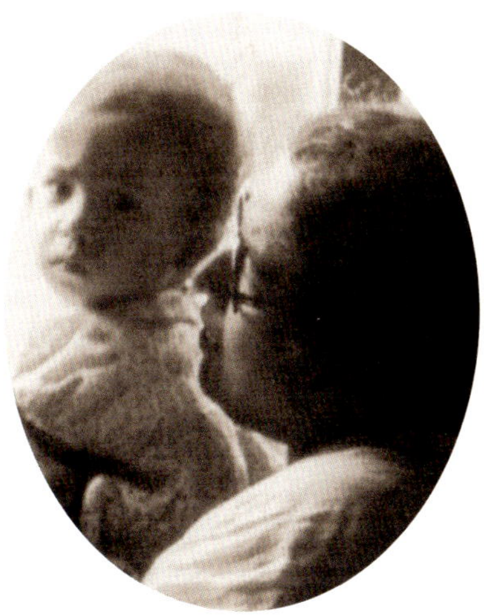

RIGHT:

The mothers and their sons.

Annapurna Devi with Subho Shankar (left) and Zubeda Khan with Dhyanesh Khan (right).

BELOW:

Doting father, dutiful daughter.

Boro Baba with daughter, Annapurna Devi.

BOTTOM:

Baba with Ameena Perera, his only granddaughter.

She plays the sitar *and now teaches in Calcutta.*

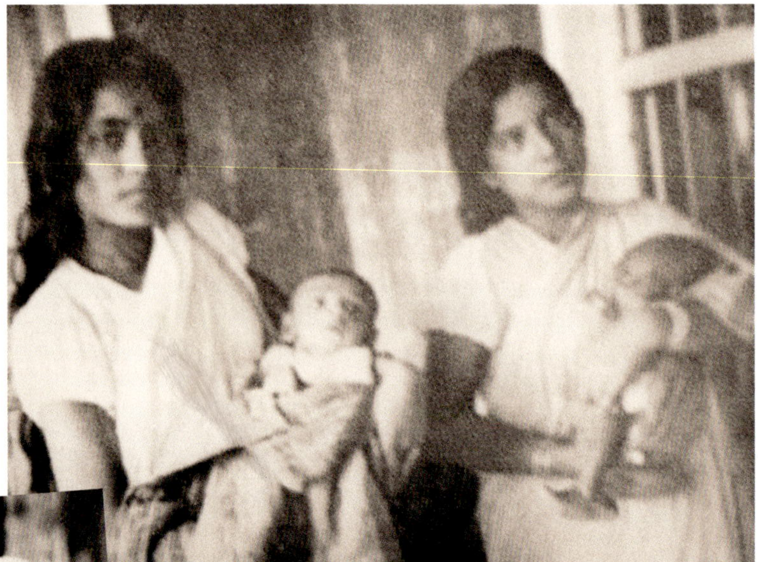

of the time when Boro Baba saw her for the first time in Bangladesh. Before she was married to my grandfather, Boro Baba came to meet her father. She did not recognize him and was sitting on the swing outside the house. Boro Baba enquired about her father and she boldly asked him who he was. Even to this day, when she recalls the incident, my grandmother bites her tongue with shame! Perhaps this innocence in her struck Boro Baba and she was chosen as his daughter-in-law. She narrates how he became a father and tutor to her. The way she has enforced her code of conduct and discipline in the house is under his tutelage. She even attributes her style of cooking to Boro Baba. Boro Baba never liked to see her

Madina Begum with her grandchildren in Maihar.

Aashish Khan on Madina Begum's extreme right and Ameena Perera on her left. Pranesh Khan can be seen standing in between Madina Begum and Ameena Perera.

or Annapurna wearing the same saree for consecutive days and if he observed such repetition, he would personally go the very next day and buy a bundle of clothes for them. The affection showered towards youngsters was not so much in words as in actions.

Boro Baba's students have always described him as a strict disciplinarian. However, my grandmother points out, had he not been an epitome of discipline and determination, it would have been impossible for him to nurture such great musicians. It is almost a proverb in the *gharana* that whomever Boro Baba touched had turned golden; he taught and his students became famous. Even at an advanced age, the strength of his voice could shatter the ego of all those around him and make anyone shiver at a single call from him. He was nearing hundred when he underwent his first surgery. My grandmother still remembers the difficult time that he gave the anaesthetists when they tried to make him unconscious. The doctors commented with surprise on the old man having such strength in his nerves.

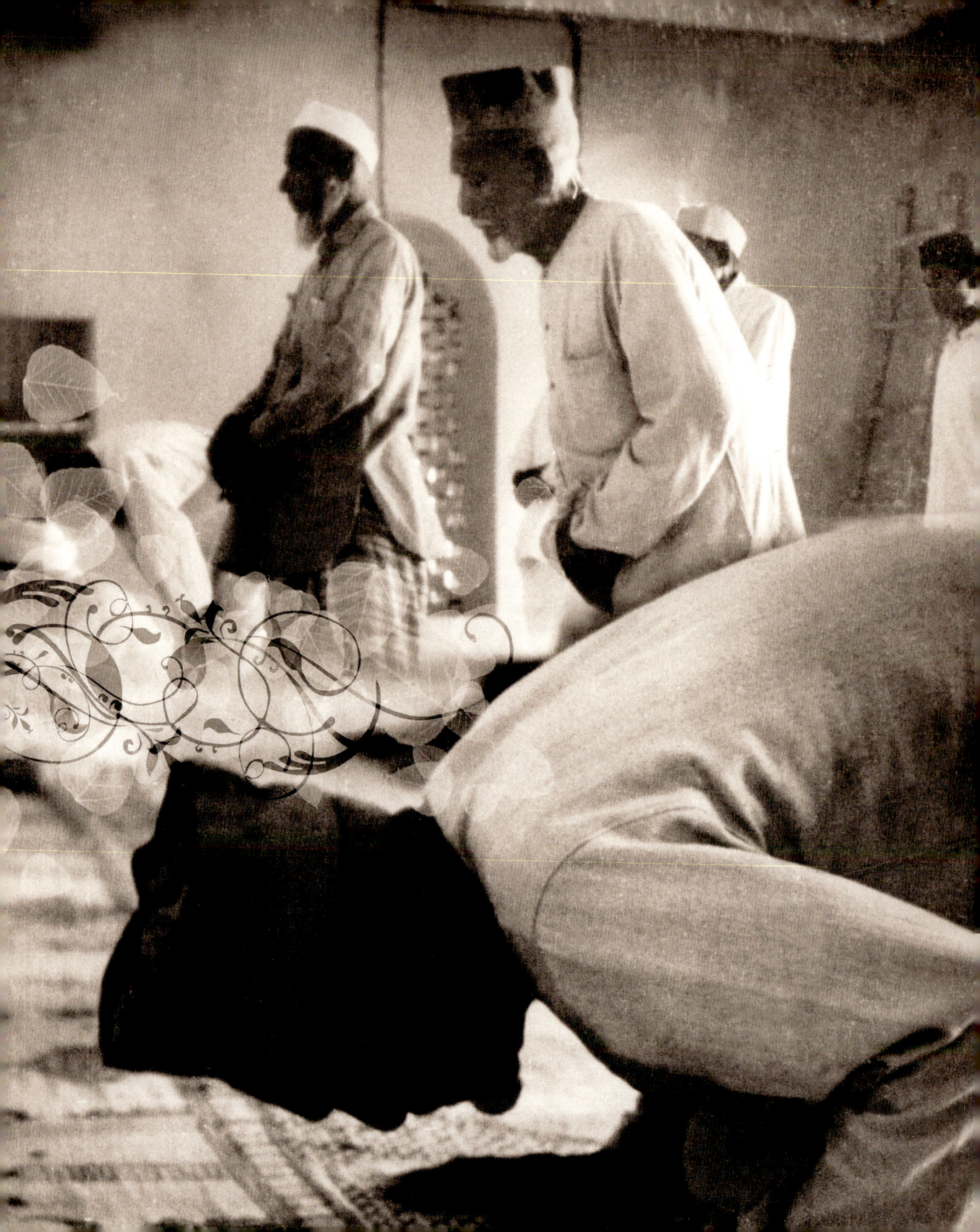

Boro Baba – The Devout

15

Our lives are the only meaningful expression of what we believe and in whom we believe. And the only real wealth, for any of us, lies in our faith.

—Gordon B. Hinckley

Boro Baba was a pious and very secular man. Though always engaged in religious thoughts, he was never bigoted. He always believed that music was a way to reach God. Boro Baba was an early riser and also read *namaz* five times a day without fail; he was a simple man who led a basic life. He strongly desired to perform Hajj and was able to do so later. It materialized in 1935–36, when he went to Bai-tul Muqqades (Mecca) while touring with Uday Shankar's troupe.

To Mecca

When Boro Baba's ship set sail from Bombay on its way to Holy Mecca, several of his fans and many renowned musicians of India were there to see him off. The luggage included his *sarode*, carefully encased in a wooden box, with his name written on it: 'Dr. Alauddin Khan'. As the ship sailed on the high seas, a funny thing happened. Several of the passengers, feeling sea-sick, came to him seeking medicine for relief. Boro Baba was surprised and said he had no knowledge of medical science. Nor was he equipped with any medicine. Then it dawned on him that they had mistaken him to be a physician fooled by the 'Doctor' preceding his name: which was an honorary degree for his contribution to music.

FACING PAGE:

Baba prostrating while reading the namaz.

Boro Baba was god-fearing and read the namaz religiously.

Boro Baba writes about his visit to the Bai-tul Muqqades in a letter to his younger brother, Ayet Ali from Tel Aviv:

'We went to Bai-tul Muqqades on January 29 (1935). I presented a show there, playing the *sarode* for an audience of 2000 people. Let me now give you the happy news. The Almighty blessed me with an opportunity to see paradise. He gave me the chance to offer prayers at His altar. No Hindu can go there and I was worried whom to take with me since all our troupe members are Hindus. On 30 January, after my morning prayers, I started for Bai-tul Muqqades all alone. Since I don't know Arabic, I couldn't ask anyone for directions. Neither do they understand Urdu. It was terrible. In the name of God, I started from my hotel. On my way, someone called me from behind. I could not understand what he said. He directed me to go with him. I wondered if he was going to kill me for money. Then I thought that even if I died in this Holy Land, it was worthwhile and followed him. After a distance (say, from Shibpur to its next village, Bidyakut), the man told me to go right and said the Mehrab Sharif was close by. I took a few steps forward and turned back – the man was nowhere to be seen! What was happening? I started to cry. God Himself had brought me here!'

Walking another 200 yards, Boro Baba reached the gate of Bai-tul Muqqades. At the entrance a *maulvi* looked at him suspiciously and asked if he was a Muslim or a Hindu. In reply, Boro Baba recited the *kalemas* and *suras* that he knew well. The *maulvi* smiled and respectfully took him to the in-charge of the shrine. After Boro Baba again recited all the *kalemas* and *suras* in reply to his queries, the in-charge asked him to go and offer his prayers. He was then taken inside the two-thousand-year-old mosque – the largest in the world. Boro Baba felt as though he were in heaven and wondered at the craftsmanship of the mosque. How many millions of devotees had offered their prayers there...then he went inside and prayed six *rakats* of *nafal*.

Pleased with Boro Baba's faith and devotion, the pesh imam himself prayed for him. Boro Baba was overjoyed to hear from him that he should be able to perform Hajj.

Ma Sharda.

This temple belongs to Ma Sharda who is considered the goddess of music. Boro Baba was an ardent follower of Ma Sharda. His secular ways are still talked about in Maihar.

The pesh imam's forecast came true – Boro Baba did perform Hajj and his dearest dream was fulfilled.

Rampur Baba, a friend of Boro Baba.

He was a saint who is said to have lived for many years.

A Devotee of Ma Sharda

Ma Sharda Devi is the presiding deity of Maihar. In the *Puranas*, she is referred to as the destroyer of the demon Moi. She is said to be an incarnation of Saraswati, the goddess of music and learning, and her idol is enshrined atop a hill in Maihar. The Maharaja of Maihar had donated money to fund an estate called the Sharda Ma estate which met the expenses of the temple and worship of the deity. Baba was a devotee of Shree Sharda Ma and firmly believed that all his prosperity was due to her blessings. He had once climbed up the 557 steps of the hill with offerings for her.

Such was his devotion and faith in Ma, that once, during a protracted illness, it was proposed that he be shifted to a hospital for treatment, but he objected. He preferred to die at Ma Sharda's feet, rather than be cured elsewhere. Today, visitors from all over the world visit Maihar and pay their homage to Ma Sharda and at Boro Baba's tomb.

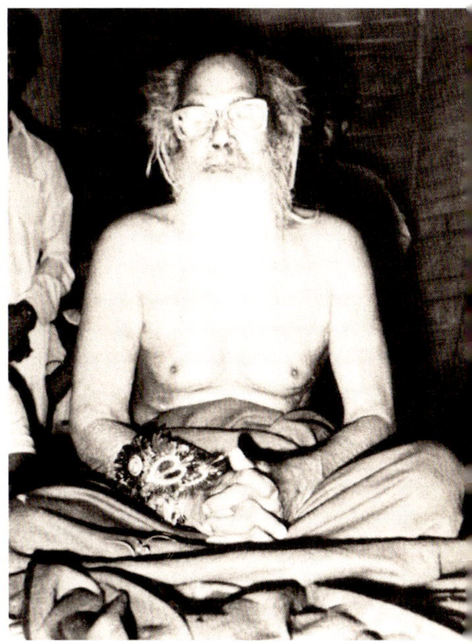

There was also the saint Rampur Baba, who is said to have lived for over a century in the hills of Maihar. He passed away in the late 1980s in Maihar. Boro Baba had great respect for him and often went for his *darshan*. Even today, our family has the same reverence for Rampur Baba and whenever we are in Maihar we visit his shrine without fail.

On a more personal note, a noted musician who Boro Baba had interacted with was Hirendra Kumar Ganguli. Popularly known as Hiru Babu, he was a barrister by profession and also a disciple of Abed Hussain Khan from 1919-36. Hiru Babu recalls meeting Boro Baba for the first time at the latter's disciple, Timir Baran's house. Boro Baba had embraced him and expressed a desire to perform with him. Later Boro Baba, Hiru Babu and Abed Hussain Khan performed at the All India Music Conference in Lucknow. On another occasion, Hiru Babu and Boro Baba were playing through the night at the

Love for all.

Boro Baba embracing a street goat in front of Golamath Shiva Temple in Maihar.

Tansen Music Conference. During the interval, Boro Baba went to read his *namaz* at around 4 a.m. Hiru Babu remembers passing by Baba and witnessing an exceptional, almost divine aura surrounding the great musician as he prayed. 'He was an *adarsha* (ideal) disciple, guru and artist, and above all, an *adarsha* human being. He never accepted any money from his disciples. Instead, he allowed them to live in his house, taught them and completed their *shiksha* according to the actual norms of the *guru-shishya parampara*... whenever he would play with Ali Akbar and Aashish Khan, it was as if Alauddin Khan was actually the youngest of the lot. It has been my privilege to accompany this legend on the tabla,' says Hiru Babu.

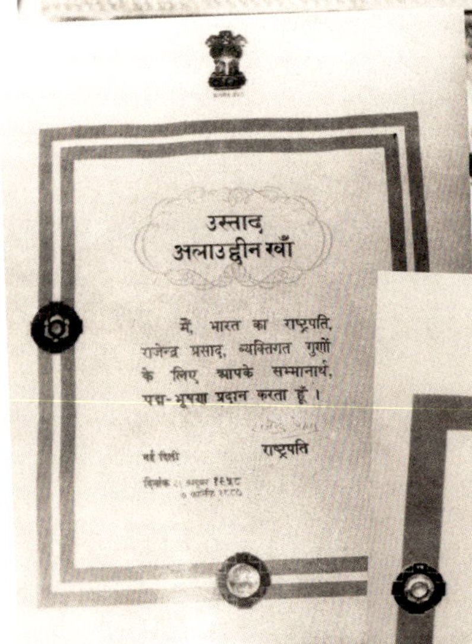

उस्ताद
अलाउद्दीन खाँ

मैं, भारत का राष्ट्रपति, राजेन्द्र प्रसाद, व्यक्तिगत गुणों के लिए आपके सम्मानार्थ, पद्म-भूषण प्रदान करता हूँ।

नई दिल्ली

राष्ट्रपति

अलाउद्दीन खाँ

मैं भारत का राष्ट्रपति, वराहगिरि वेंकट गिरि, व्यक्तिगत गुणों के लिए आपके सम्मानार्थ, पद्म विभूषण प्रदान करता हूँ।

नई दिल्ली

राष्ट्रपति

The awards.

TOP:

Receiving the Padma Bhushan from President Rajendra Prasad in 1958.

MIDDLE:

The Padma Bhushan awarded to Boro Baba in 1958.

BOTTOM:

The Padma Vibhushan awarded to Boro Baba in 1971.

Epilogue

After having contributed immensely to mankind's musical treasure for nearly a century, Boro Baba breathed his last in Maihar on September 6, 1972. He left behind a greatly enriched tradition of music which has since been passed down generations of music lovers, keeping his memory alive.

He never lusted after material gain or fame. He always wanted to learn and to create; qualities that took him to eminence. It is a sad fact that in the world of contemporary Indian classical music, not enough is remembered of the fundamental contributions he made to evolve its tradition and enable subsequent generations to carry on. Music is said to be immortal – it continues to exist and flourish well past its creators. While on one hand, Ustad Alauddin Khan forged new ways of taking the rich Indian classical tradition to the masses in his homeland, on the other hand, he took it beyond its boundaries – to its rightful place on the world stage.

He was known for his improvisations, his exceptional qualities of freshness and proportion and his exquisite tone production technique, which he continued to refine until his death. Moreover, the style of playing he developed is a virtual reference for musicians of the present generation. A *sarode* virtuoso of the highest order, his consistently brilliant and exciting performances not only established him as a national treasure, but also earned him worldwide recognition and acclaim in the form of prestigious awards. Some of these awards are the Sangeet Natak Academy Award (1952), Sangeet Acharya Award from Indrakala Sangeet Vishwavidyalya, Khairagarh (1961), the Padma Bhushan (1958), the Doctorate of Literature Award from Rabindra Bharati University, Calcutta (1963), the title of Vadya Acharya from Bhatkhande University of Music, Lucknow (1944)

Boro Baba in a concert with his students.

Boro Baba with Hirendra Kumar Ganguli on the tabla, *Ali Akbar Khan on the* sarode *and Dhyanesh Khan on the* tanpura.

and the Desikottam, an honorary doctorate from Vishwa Bharati University, Shanti Niketan. In 1971, he received India's second highest civilian award, the Padma Vibhushan.

Once in a while, there emerges a great musician who, through his genius, ignites a certain spark, necessary to elevate an instrument to another level of expression and appreciation. For the *sarode*, it was Ustad Alauddin Khan. He breathed new life into the instrument and conferred upon it a stature and respect, never before enjoyed. The brightest disciple of the Senia *gharana* was, in his lifetime, the most celebrated exponent of this style. It is through his beloved music, that Ustad Alauddin Khan the legend, lives on.

Boro Baba with some other renowned names of music.

TOP:

(L to R): Ariyakudi Ramanuja Iyengar, Karaikudi Sambasivan Iyer, Ustad Mushtaq Hussain and Ustad Alauddin Khan

BOTTOM:

Ustad Alauddin Khan with Bade Ghulam Ali.

Glossary

Alaap	:	Un-metered raga introduction and expansion; prelude.
Bhajan	:	Devotional song.
Bol(s)	:	Sound syllables as in tabla bols; differ for every instrument.
Dadra	:	A light classical song; thumri type; sung in a time cycle of six beats (3 + 3).
Drut	:	Fast tempo or laya. It is performed after the madhya-laya (medium tempo) and marks the climax of the performance.
Gat	:	Rhythmic composition in instrumental music.
Gharana	:	A school of music representing a specific musical lineage or tradition and an individualistic style of rendering.
Manjari	:	Collection, bouquet.
Meend	:	Smooth gliding movement between two swaras.
Pandit	:	Generally a Hindu title meaning learned man; scholar.
Parampara	:	Guru-Shishya Parampara or the sacred relationship between the master and the pupil by which knowledge is transmitted to the next generation.
Raga	:	Modal scale.
Sadhana	:	Means of attainment; self-realization through any medium, musical or spiritual.
Sangeet	:	Musical science.
Sargam	:	The seven notes (swaras) of the scale; name derived from the first four notes (Sa, Re, Ga, Ma).
Shruti	:	Micro tone, or a micro tonal interval.
Swara	:	Musical note.
Sur	:	Tone, pitch or note.
Tala	:	A time cycle, a rhythm structure and a measure applied in the act of keeping time.
Taleem	:	Training/instruction in Urdu.
Tarana	:	A style of singing.
Ustad	:	Muslim title meaning master.
Vilambit	:	Slow tempo. The charm of vilambit is in grave, temperate sweetness.